The Orchard

The Orchard

A Memoir

THERESA WEIR

GRAND CENTRAL
PUBLISHING

NEW YORK   BOSTON

Grand Central Publishing
Hachette Book Group
237 Park Avenue
New York, NY 10017

www.HachetteBookGroup.com

Printed in the United States of America

First Edition: September 2011
10 9 8 7 6 5 4 3 2 1

Grand Central Publishing is a division of Hachette Book Group, Inc.
The Grand Central Publishing name and logo is a trademark of Hachette Book Group, Inc.

The publisher is not responsible for websites (or their content) that are not owned by the publisher.

Library of Congress Cataloging-in-Publication Data

Weir, Theresa, 1954–
    The orchard / Theresa Weir.—1st ed.
      p. cm.
    ISBN 978-0-446-58469-2
    1. Weir, Theresa, 1954– 2. Authors, American—21st century—
Biography. I. Title.
PS3573.E3976Z46 2011
813'.6—dc22
[B]
                                                        2011001849

For my children

Author's Note

A variety of apple called Sweet Melinda did not exist. The Sweet Melindas' story in this book symbolizes the old and original orchard, hand planted by my husband's great-grandfather over a hundred years ago and eventually destroyed by the codling moth. All of the scenes featuring the Sweet Melindas were drawn from the real-life drama and struggle to save the old orchard, which wasn't as disease- and insect-resistant as the young orchard with its newer dwarf trees.

Names in *The Orchard* have been changed to protect the privacy of individuals, and Connie and Boyd are composites. In some places, the sequences of events have been changed, events combined, and timelines condensed for the sake of story flow. The standard farming practices described in this book took place over fifteen years ago, and the author has no knowledge of practices since that time.

The Orchard

The Legend of Lily

Lily's father sold herbicide and pesticide to farmers. She sometimes came into contact with the world of farming, but never the actual soil and crops. Never the tractors or plows. No, only with the mysterious liquid her father sold in giant drums and big plastic jugs.

The child knew her dad sold important stuff that people needed to farm, but beyond that, she really didn't care.

"If I sell enough this summer, I could win us a free trip to Disneyland," the father told his daughter.

Lily sat in the passenger seat of the Monte Carlo as they headed for their third stop of the day. She hardly ever got a chance to sit in front, and it made her feel important and grown-up.

The windows were down, and Lily's hair stung her face. Every so often, she would glance at her dad's profile as he smoked and talked. He wore a new plaid shirt with short sleeves, and he smelled nice because of the aftershave he'd put on before they'd left the house.

"What kind of rides do they have at Disneyland?" she asked.

"Everything," her dad said. "Everything you can think of. Boats that go through jungles, and caves with pirates. But my sales have to be good. You'll help me with that today, won't you?"

Lily nodded and bounced her legs in a sudden burst of enthusiasm.

She was seven, and her feet didn't quite touch the floor. "I'll help you, Daddy."

He reached across the seat and squeezed her arm. "Of course you will. You're my girl." They were a team.

Soon Lily's father pulled the car around to the back door of the VFW, and Lily helped him unload. Dusty pickup trucks filled the lot. The VFW buildings they visited all looked the same. The ceilings were low and the lights were fluorescent. Long, narrow rooms with wood paneling on the walls. Flags on metal stands. Pictures of men in uniforms.

Eventually everyone sat down on folding chairs, and Lily's father moved to the front of the room and began talking to the crowd of mostly men. Lily watched, amazed, because he suddenly seemed like somebody from television, like somebody who was on the news. Somebody she would believe and trust. Not that she didn't trust him. She did, but this was different. He was her dad, but not her dad.

Lily didn't understand a lot of what he said. He seemed so smart as he told them about *his product*. One of the things he talked about was how safe it was. The safest on the market.

Lily had brought her crayons, and her father had given her a sheet of paper that advertised the herbicide. Even though she'd turned it over, she could still see the design through the paper. She tried to pretend it wasn't there, concentrating on drawing a house and family.

Some of the letters became part of the house's roof. Lily pressed harder on the crayon, trying to cover up the design. Beyond the world of crayons and paper, she heard her dad telling things to the men.

He talked for a while, saying stuff about broad-spectrum herbicides and incentives. "I've got a ten-minute presentation I hope you'll watch," he finally said. "That will be followed by a demonstration I guarantee will sell you on our product if the film doesn't do it for you."

The lights were shut off, and Lily had to stop coloring.

She understood very little of the film, but a man's voice used words she'd often heard her father use. Words like *carryover* and *drift*. Words you'd probably want to hear if you were a farmer and you wanted to kill weeds. Her father had told her that farmers couldn't use the same kind of herbicide on all plants, and if they used certain stuff on corn one year, they might not be able to plant beans in that same field the next year. Which was why carryover was important. It made her feel special to know these words.

The heat, the fans, the dark room, and the hum of the projector caused Lily to fall asleep and stay asleep until she felt someone shaking her arm. Confused, she lifted her head and blinked, trying to focus.

The film was over, and the lights were on. Lily's dad gave her a smile, then turned back to the crowd.

"At our company, we're concerned about the farmer and the consumer," he told them. "We care about the environment, and our products are safe. In fact, our new herbicide is as safe as drinking water. Safer than some drinking water, when you consider the number of wells contaminated with parasites and bacteria."

That got a laugh from the men.

He popped the top on a gallon pesticide container. He poured clear liquid into a clear glass. He brought the glass to his lips, swallowed the contents, then held the empty glass high. "Safe enough to drink."

Then he poured again and offered the glass to Lily.

"I'm not thirsty," she said.

People laughed, but it was a nervous laugh.

"Come on." Now she heard the command in his voice.

The contents of the glass looked like water, but it smelled like the trunk of her dad's car. It was an odor she associated with him. An odor she could sometimes smell on his breath.

"Drink it." He smiled, but the smile didn't reach his eyes.

Lily took the glass. It wasn't full. It wasn't even half full.

At that point, Lily became aware of the silence in the room. She looked around, and it seemed like every person in the building was staring at her.

"Tastes like soda," her dad whispered.

He was lying. Lily knew he was lying.

She lifted the glass to her mouth and drank. Fast.

It burned all the way down, and when it hit bottom, Lily's stomach clenched and she struggled to keep the chemicals from coming up. It was like drinking fire. But they were a team and she wanted to go to Disneyland.

She wiped her mouth with the back of her hand and smiled.

"Good?" her father asked.

She bobbed her head. Then, with her belly burning, she gathered up her picture and crayons while the men in the room placed their orders.

The Courtship

CHAPTER ONE

Burlington, Iowa, 1963

They say that as soon as we're born we begin to die. I hadn't spent much time thinking about death until I was eight and a neighbor lady brought over a bunch of mushrooms. They looked like white toadstools. Some were freshly picked, with black dirt clinging to their pulpy roots. Some were fried. No other adults were around as she crouched and lowered the plate to my level.

"Have one, Theresa. I'm sure your mother won't mind."

She smelled like soap and clothes that had just been ironed. She wore pink lipstick, yellow beachcombers, and white sandals. She was so unlike the moody women in my family.

I ate a mushroom.

Later my mother and aunt put their dark heads together and whispered their concerns about the food.

They could be poisonous.

Oh yes, they look poisonous.

A book on edible and inedible mushrooms materialized, and soon the neighbor's gift was declared lethal. An innocent but serious mistake.

It seemed that the simple act of placing your hand to your mouth after touching one could bring about violent death within hours.

I didn't tell anyone that my life was over. Instead I went to my room, lay down on the bed, and waited to die.

Waiting to die is strange no matter your age. If I'd mentioned the ingested mushroom to anyone, I'm sure I would have felt just as alone.

I mentally went through the list of symptoms.

Rapid heartbeat. Yes.

Sweating. Yes.

Dizziness. Yes.

I expected to hear an ambulance come roaring up the hill to collect the neighbor and her family. But if everybody in their house had eaten the poison mushrooms, no one would be able to call for help. Maybe they were all unconscious. Or dead, and we would soon catch whiffs of their bloated carcasses.

That night I didn't sleep, and when I got up the next day, I opened the mushroom book, which had been left on the table, and revisited the symptoms. Fear made me weak.

"Are you feeling okay?" my mother asked, more with annoyance than with maternal concern. If I told her I was dying, she would get mad, because almost everything I did made her angry. Two years had passed since my father had left us. Once he was gone, he was gone. No phone calls. No letters. No visits. He just walked out the door and never looked back. "He didn't want kids," my mother later explained. I was relieved to discover he disliked kids in general and that his disappearance wasn't caused by anything I'd done.

"I'm okay," I said, and hurried from the house. In an attempt to distract myself, I crossed the street to a friend's. She got out a board game, but when my plastic game piece ended in the Land of Poison Toadstools, I had to leave without explanation.

Outside, I spotted the neighbor woman in her straw sun hat and gardening gloves and blond loveliness. She gave me a happy wave, looking very much alive.

Death will occur within hours.

I gave her a wave back, much happier to see her than she was to see me.

What if time wasn't linear? If you were to draw a line on a piece of paper, then fold that paper, the day I ate the mushroom would touch the future. Maybe the future was what I'd really felt.

I would live. But the mushroom incident set up a theme that would continue for the rest of my life, an acute awareness of human fragility and the knowledge that, consciously or subconsciously, we are all at the mercy of our fears, and we are all waiting to die.

CHAPTER TWO

Henderson County, Illinois, 1975

A farmer dressed in denim overalls took a seat at the bar. "Bottle of Blue."

We served two kinds of beer, Blue Ribbon and Budweiser. All in bottles, nothing on tap. I opened the bottle and put down a cardboard coaster with a glass.

The bar was located on the ridge of what locals called the bottoms, where, before dams, the river had been miles wide and the fertile soil left behind was rich, almost too dense to cut with a plow blade. On a winter day, when the sun hit that shiny black gumbo, you could smell the river that used to be there.

Outside, the wind raged across ground that had been deliberately stripped bare of trees and fences. Through the glass double doors, the air was a yellow haze, and I could smell the chemicals from the fields. The man in front of me gave off a hint of something like garlic. I could taste it whenever he shifted his weight.

The scent recalled the story farmers told about a girl named Lily whose father made her drink herbicide. As it was with all tales passed from person to person, no one knew if the girl and the salesman really existed. While working in the bar, I'd heard various versions, and I never missed the opportunity to ask if the storyteller had ever seen the child or the father.

The answer tended to be variations of the same. "No, but my brother did." "No, but my uncle did." Always someone related who'd been there, who'd seen it, but I'd never spoken to an actual eyewitness and had finally come to the conclusion that the story was an urban legend that was rural, perhaps started by a rival herbicide salesman, or possibly an environmental group.

The farmer lit a cigarette. His arms were coated with a fine layer of powder that he was too exhausted to notice.

He came here a lot because only a truck stop and a gravel road separated his land and the bar. He could park his tractor and walk straight from the field. He was shy and polite, but I was an outsider. If I lived here fifty more years, I would still be an outsider.

Business was slow for a Saturday, and he hoped more farmers would show up so he had someone else to talk to. For his sake, I hoped so too.

Fatigue threatened to press him to the floor, but he made an attempt at polite conversation. "Windy."

I looked through the doors and lifted my eyebrows in surprise, as if I hadn't noticed. "Wow."

He wouldn't complain. He wouldn't tell me that he'd just spent the last twelve hours on an old tractor with no cab.

He poured beer into the short glass and took a swallow. "Nice and cool in here."

I did a mental shift as his words reminded me that it was spring outside. And hot. And even more unpleasant out there than inside the bar.

At that point, I realized the poor man had reached a mind-set I could only dream of achieving. I was almost jealous, and I wondered what it would be like to live in his skin.

The farmer slid some coins across the top of the bar. His square-tipped fingers were cracked and dry, and I imagined they would feel like rough sandpaper. "Get yourself a beer."

I glanced at the clock. A little past six.

Eight o'clock. That was my target. But I rarely lasted that long.

When I unlocked the front door and flipped on the OPEN sign, I always swore I wouldn't drink that day. But somebody usually ended up buying me a beer. And another. We didn't have a dishwasher, so the glasses were sterilized in a bleach bath. I loved that hint of bleach mixed with beer. A whiff of bleach and I was licking my lips.

My drinking was justified, because if I got drunk enough I would perch at the end of the bar and entertain customers with my acoustic guitar and halfway-decent voice, my repertoire consisting of Creedence Clearwater Revival, Neil Young, Cat Stevens, and a few songs of my own.

"Thanks." I smiled, put the money in the register, and served myself a beer, wondering if it was possible to be an alcoholic at twenty-one.

I came from a long line of people who embraced suffering and angst and their own dark nature while trying to drown it with anything that could numb the mind. Forget my mother, who'd been known to rant and wail: "Oh, I wish I were dead!" My uncle was the master. My mother had been way too melodramatic and heavy-handed. My uncle's technique was subtle, and he wore his cloak of despair in silence. I liked that.

There was something infinitely reassuring in knowing things couldn't get any worse. There was a comfort in not waiting to fall and not waiting to get knocked down. If you have vertigo, you want to be on the ground, not climbing a tower. This might explain how, at the ripe age of twenty, I'd joined my uncle in his cornfield bar along a sad, lonely stretch of highway not far from the Mississippi River.

I was in training.

Behind the hard liquor, on a narrow shelf just for display, were my uncle's Avon figurine decanters. Cats and pheasants and ladies in long dresses, all covered in a layer of dust. He was the local Avon representative, and farm wives would slink into the bar to place their orders. Sometimes they sat on stools and bought a glass of soda, but never once had I seen any of them order alcohol.

Avon wasn't my uncle's only side business. He hid flat movie-reel boxes out back behind the bar. Shady characters took the boxes and left payment in a coffee can. The only reason I knew about it was because one of the shady guys had come into the bar, leaned close, and told me he was there to rent porn.

"Porn!" I'd been outraged. "We don't rent porn here!" This was a family bar.

A couple of regulars had coughed in their hands and stared into their beers. Uncle Jim had appeared out of nowhere and given the guy a few strange eye signals, and they'd vanished together.

I'd felt like such an idiot once the truth was out. And I'd felt like an even bigger idiot once I realized everybody else knew about his little 35 mm side business.

But that didn't keep it from adding another layer of scum to my life. And it bothered me that I actually lived in a bar where porn was sold under the table. Or in this case, out behind the building.

An hour later, the bell above the door jingled. The farmer was gone, and I'd finished my beer.

This customer was a regular named Larry. He had his whole family with him. His bleach-blond pregnant wife and three dirty, barefoot kids.

The alarming thing is that I was glad to see Larry and his wife and kids.

That's what happened when you lived smack dab in the middle of bleak. Pretty soon everybody and everything became normal. Pretty soon it didn't seem bleak. People adapt. But that bit of self-preservation could turn on you when you took it too far. Pretty soon you started thinking everything was fine and you lost all desire to do anything but sit around and shoot the shit with people like Larry.

This was my future. My future was a bell and the people who walked through that door.

Larry hefted the kids on bar stools and ordered a round of Stewart's sandwiches—little prepackaged hamburgers heated in a small oven. They were good the way fake food was good.

The kids were already crying and fighting. I felt sorry for them and disgusted by them at the same time.

"I'm thirsty," one of them whined. They all had white hair and blue scalp veins that just begged to be poked with a finger.

"Can they have some water?" Larry asked.

My uncle and I looked at the sign on the wall, put in place by the health department. The drinking water was unfit for children because of high nitrate levels. And if nitrates were in the water, no telling what other toxins were in there.

Which was why I stuck with beer.

My uncle opened the upright cooler and pulled a gallon of milk from the shelf he stocked with a few staples. He lined up three short beer glasses, filled them, and nudged the glasses toward the kids. "On the house."

The pregnant wife was putting balls on the pool table. "Let's play a game, Larry."

"Not now, babe."

"Oh, come on. One game."

Larry had his elbows on the bar, his back to his wife. Weight of the world and all that. The kids finished off their milk, gummed up the sandwiches, and jumped to the floor, where they scuffled in front of the wooden rack that held the pool cues.

The door jangled again.

I looked up, expecting a different version of Larry. But this was someone new. Someone I'd never seen in the bar before.

I could hear the kids yammering away. Peripherally I saw one of them peek over the edge of the pool table and reach for the cue ball with one gooey hand.

My uncle was laid-back, but he didn't like kids using the table. Right now, though, he was focused on the man who'd just stepped in the door.

The jukebox was playing, and the kids continued to yammer. Larry leaned across the bar. "You know who that is, don't you?" His voice was a harsh whisper, and his eyes had that gossip glint. "Adrian Curtis." Larry poured the rest of his beer into his glass. "His grandfather died of cancer a few months ago." He inched even closer. "Some people say his farm is cursed."

Adrian Curtis took a seat at a table on the opposite side of the bar, in front of the window.

I shrugged. "A lot of people die of cancer."

"Yeah, but the grandfather also lost three kids, two in a freak accident. And then there's the worker who had the tractor roll over on him. Crushed to death."

On her way around the pool table, Larry's wife paused to join the conversation. "And what about the guy who hung himself?"

"He didn't do that on the farm," Larry said. "That was later. After he moved away."

"Like a week later."

Larry glanced over his shoulder. There was no way the man in the corner could hear him—the music was too loud. "You know that missing woman from Oquawka? The one they're still looking for? Police called in a psychic from the Quad Cities." Larry laughed quietly. "You believe that? Psychic kept saying she saw a woman's body in a grove of trees. Kept talking about straight rows of trees. Police looked all over Curtis Orchard but never found nothin'."

"You really think the farm is cursed?" I asked.

"I don't know." Larry took a swallow of beer. "It's just weird. That's all. Weird. A lot of people connected to the place have died. That's all I'm sayin'."

My uncle picked up Larry's empty bottle and placed it in the plastic tub under the counter. With a bar cloth, he wiped up an imaginary spill. "I'll wait on him."

"That's okay." I grabbed the round plastic tray with its nonslip liner. "I'll do it."

"You don't have to."

"What do you think he's going to do? Put a curse on me?"

Larry laughed, and my uncle responded with a weak smile. I was the kid he'd never had, and he tended to be overprotective in odd ways.

At the table, I braced the tray against my stomach, setting an ashtray and coaster in front of the man named Adrian Curtis. He was the most handsome farmer I'd ever seen in my life, with light curls, a square jaw, bleached brows over eyes as blue as a Billie Holiday song. I planned to treat him the same as any other customer, but it would be hard.

He hadn't come from the field. Instead of denim and dust, he wore black pants and a crisp white shirt. "Wedding or funeral?" I asked.

He blinked, as if noticing me for the first time.

People say I remind them of Audrey Hepburn. I've never seen the resemblance other than my short dark hair. I know my features can be a bit startling, with big eyes in a small face, but some guys occasionally find me attractive. I'd never really cared before. I always liked booze more than I liked guys, but my heart was suddenly beating a little faster than usual, and the air was spiked.

"Wedding."

"You don't sound happy. Weddings are supposed to be happy."

He seemed caught off guard; then a reluctant smile touched his lips. "It brought back some memories—that's all."

His voice was exactly what I thought it would be. Smooth and mellow.

"I hope you at least got some cake."

Whenever I stood on the edge of anything high, I always wanted to close my eyes, spread my arms, and fall forward. Did everybody feel that way? We spend our days struggling to stay alive, but the second we're put on the edge of a cliff, we want to jump.

"So what can I get you?" I asked, watching as he tapped a cigarette from a new pack.

"Whatever you have on draft."

"We only serve bottle beer." I rattled off our two selections.

He patted his shirt, his hands searching for a pocket that didn't exist. I grabbed a book of matches from my tray and held them out to him. Our fingers brushed. "Thanks." He lit his cigarette, and I noticed his lips were full and sensual.

"What?" He'd caught me staring.

"Nothing." I felt heat rise in my face and wondered if I'd ever reach a point in my life when I no longer blushed. No matter how cool I played it, blushing always gave me away. I shook my head. "Nothing. It's just been a strange day."

He smiled. "Oh, yeah. Tell me about it."

A song finished playing, and the bottom dropped out of the room.

Behind me, the kids were arguing and balls were clacking. From outside came the sound of traffic. Through the window, I saw my uncle standing under the big road sign. He flipped the switch and most of the lights came on.

Pilot House.

I hadn't been crazy about the name, but it was a fitting nod to the barges that carried grain and coal up and down the Mississippi River, which flowed on the other side of the levee. Before it was the Pilot House it had been the Coach and Four Lounge. Before that, it had been my maternal grandmother's home until her death. Adrian Curtis now sat in the approximate area of the living room where years ago on Christmas Eve I'd opened a little china tea set decorated with delicate pink roses.

Right now I prayed there was still a song left on the jukebox, something that would fill the empty spots in the room. I heard a series of familiar mechanical clicks as one record was replaced by another. Music filled the space once more, making everything better.

"Get yourself a beer too. If you drink."

Did I ever.

I felt a giggle rise in me, and I struggled to hold it down. Once those things got started… "Thanks." I ducked my head, spun on my heel, and hurried behind the bar to fill his order.

Larry and his wife were in a huddle. "Wasn't he supposed to marry somebody and they broke it off at the last minute?" she whispered.

Larry nodded. "I heard she dumped him."

"I heard *he* dumped *her*. Probably got sick of her. You'd never get sick of me, would you, babe?" Larry's wife asked.

I pulled a beer from the cooler and closed the curved, stainless-steel lid, then hooked the bottle under the metal opener, popped the top, turned a glass upside down on the neck, and carried the cold drink to Adrian.

He didn't look up. "I should be used to it by now," he said.

"Used to what?"

Elbow on the table, he removed the glass and lifted the beer bottle to his mouth, then placed it on the coaster. "People talking about me."

"Nobody…" I stopped my obvious lie before I embarrassed myself more. "I didn't think you could hear us."

"I couldn't. It's the body language that always gives it away."

"Sorry."

"Did you get yourself a beer?"

"You still want to buy me one?"

"Sure. Why not? But you have to sit here and drink it with me."

I thought about my uncle and his porn. Sometimes people got the wrong idea about me. "I can't." I pulled back on the friendly demeanor. "I'm working."

"I didn't mean to imply anything." He flicked the ash from his cigarette and gave me a level look.

It was a cliché, but people come into bars and just start talking about things they wouldn't tell their best friends or their family. It's not the alcohol, because some customers dive in before they take that first sip. Subconsciously, they're on a therapeutic mission.

"It's just been a long time since I talked to someone about anything other than apples and weather and crops. It seems I only leave the farm for weddings and funerals."

"How do you know I won't talk about crops and rain?"

"Because you aren't from around here. I can tell. And I'd really like to talk to somebody who isn't from around here." He smiled, and I smiled in return.

"Someone with news of the outside?" I pulled out a chair and sat down. "I can tell you that people are zipping around in flying cars. And that three-pill meal? It's now a reality. So if you have vertigo and you like to eat, you haven't missed anything."

He was staring like I'd said something really interesting, which wasn't the case. I could do better.

"What's your name?"

I told him.

"That's one of my favorites."

I didn't believe him. "My brothers and I were all named after saints."

The chimes above the door sounded, and my uncle stepped back inside. I could feel his disapproval even though he was clear across the room.

I got to my feet, chair scraping. "I have to go."

"What time do you get off work?"

I was already walking away. His words stopped me. At the same time, my mind struggled to figure out what he wanted, what he was really after. I wasn't his type. I knew I wasn't his type. "Never," I heard myself saying. "I never get off."

He laughed as if my answer was the most entertaining thing he'd heard in years. And maybe it was.

"I can't believe you were so friendly to him," my uncle said once all the customers had left, including Adrian Curtis. "You don't want to get mixed up with a guy like that."

"How am I getting mixed up with him? I served him a couple beers."

"I saw the way he was looking at you. He'll be back."

"He's a farmer." Not that I had anything against farmers, but I couldn't see myself hanging out with one. "He won't be back."

"Wait and see," my uncle said.

CHAPTER THREE

A few hours later we closed for the night. I turned off the lights inside and out while my uncle removed the cash register drawer and left for his trailer behind the bar. Once the place was shut down, I opened the sofa bed in the lounge and was ready to slip out of my jeans when I heard a faint tapping. I peeked around the corner.

The bar always seemed strange at night, like a sleeping giant, full of shadows that made the familiar unfamiliar.

Someone was standing in front of the glass double doors.

I couldn't make out any features, but I knew it was Adrian Curtis.

After a brief hesitation, I crossed the room and unlocked the door.

"Do you like horses?" he asked.

Was he drunk? He'd had only two beers at our bar, but maybe he'd stopped somewhere else. "I'm still waiting for that birthday pony," I said, "so I'll say yes."

"Want to go for a ride?"

"On a horse?" I was having trouble connecting the dots.

"Yeah."

"*Now?*"

It was after two. Not that I adhered to any conventional or unconventional bedtime, but you just didn't ride horses at two a.m.

"The moon is bright. I thought it might be a nice night for it."

I was talking to a total stranger, and I could sense the instant he understood my hesitation. Even in the dark, I saw him straighten and mentally withdraw.

This moment was important, and if I rejected him I might never see him again. I thought about closing the door. Then I thought about going to bed in the lounge just a few feet from the men's restroom and urinal. "Sure. I'll come." What did I have to lose?

I found my keys, locked up behind us, and went with him.

"Where are these horses?" I asked once we were in his truck, heading down the highway.

"Horse. One horse. And he's on my farm."

One horse. I tried to construct the scene. Would we take turns? I was familiar with the way guys liked to teach women to play pool, leaning over, wrapping their arms around the girl, who would laugh and pretend she didn't know what was going on. Was this like that? Would we ride double?

Was there really a horse at all?

In the glow of Adrian's cigarette and the truck's dashboard, I noticed he was still wearing his dress clothes. Not exactly riding attire. Had he been sitting outside waiting for the bar to close? Maybe waiting for me to leave? The idea was unsettling.

Going with a stranger—*any* stranger—to the middle of nowhere was a stupid thing to do.

I block out bad memories. I pretend bad things never happened to me. That's how I cope. That's how I get by, and it's worked pretty well. But sometimes old memories surface when I least expect them. Sometimes a situation or a smell or a melody brings them back. Brings them crashing down.

Now a ride in the middle of the night with a potentially dangerous stranger reminded me of another night, a night I hadn't thought about in years. And sitting in the passenger seat of Adrian Curtis's truck, I found myself fumbling for the door handle. "You know, I didn't realize how late it was." I struggled to keep the panic from my voice. "I have to get up early tomorrow." That was a bad lie coming from someone who worked in a bar. "Don't *you* have to get up early?"

"I don't need much sleep."

Rapid heartbeat. Yes.

Sweating. Yes.

Dizziness. Yes.

"Take me home. I've changed my mind." I cringed at how pathetic I sounded.

"We're almost there." He'd barely finished the sentence when he turned off the highway. We dipped down a narrow lane, tree branches above us blocking the moon. It was a road I'd been on before. So strange...surreal to be traveling down it now with Adrian Curtis.

He stopped the truck at a metal gate. I'd expected a barn or corral, but the twin headlight beams illuminated nothing but pasture and timber. Beyond the beams, I could fill in the blanks with only my imagination.

"Have you ever been around horses?" he asked.

My heart was hammering, and my mouth had gone dry. "Some." Enough to know you didn't ride in the dark.

Adrian shut off the headlights, cut the engine, and got out. I stayed in the truck. The keys swung in the ignition, and I imagined sliding across the seat and driving off. Through the windshield, I watched Adrian climb the gate, hook his heels on a crossbar, and whistle.

Moments later, through the open passenger window, I heard the soft thud of hooves beating against the ground. Suddenly a horse burst from the darkness, blowing air out its nostrils. I could see an outline against the deep blue-black of the sky.

The horse was real.

I got out of the truck.

It was like finding that birthday pony tethered in my front yard against all odds and all expectations.

I didn't trust men. I wanted to trust them because I knew there must be some good men in the world, but the ones I'd known had lied to my face while plotting acts of violence. Women could be bitches, but men were the ones who seemed the most capable of crimes without mercy.

The smell of the horse's hair and the soft nicker, like muffled conversation, the nudge of hello and the heat of its body when I leaned over the gate and put out my hand to pat a chest of rounded muscle, all brought me reassurance.

The horse was real.

Adrian had told me the truth.

I suppose it was a testament to how messed up I was, but in those few minutes, by simply not trying to trick me, by not lying to me, by not having an ulterior motive or evil, hidden agenda, he'd gained a little of my trust, though nobody would ever have it all.

Adrian coaxed the horse close, swung his leg over, and mounted. No bridle, no saddle. Dressed in black pants and a white shirt.

"What's his name?" I asked.

Adrian was quiet a moment, and I got the idea he was deciding upon a name at that very moment. "Mr. Red."

I laughed. "A horse is a horse, of course, of course."

Mr. Red shifted and snorted, eager to move, eager to carry Adrian away. "Stand on the gate," he told me. "Yeah, like that. Put your left foot on top of mine and swing your right leg over."

I stood on the gate, and he grabbed my arm and helped me up behind him.

I'd always shunned dates with flowers and dinner and movies. That kind of thing had never been a part of my life. It was something other people did—the kind of people I didn't know and didn't understand—so I was surprised to find that such a romantic gesture as a moonlit ride on a horse appealed to me.

The animal moved slowly and surely through the dark. I trusted it. More than I trusted the man in front of me, the man I was now clinging to.

CHAPTER FOUR

The next day, not even twenty-four hours after our moonlight ride, Adrian showed up at the trailer behind the bar where my uncle and I were peeling boiled eggs for pickling.

I answered the knock to find Adrian standing at the bottom of the steps while I stood above him in the open door. He was dressed in faded jeans and a flannel shirt with the sleeves rolled a couple of turns.

"Would you like to go do something?" he asked. "Maybe a hike through the woods?"

I looked over my shoulder at my uncle. He'd stopped peeling and was staring at me. He mouthed the words *bad idea*, then dropped his egg in the gallon jar of vinegar.

"I'll be back by four." I slammed the door and hurried down the steps.

A half hour later, we were back on Adrian's farm.

We parked the truck inside a gate and hiked through a rolling pasture to finally stop on a hillside cloaked in dense trees and lush spring grass. We explored land that was too wild and steep to tame with a chainsaw and plow. Dark, secret places where deep fissures split the ground, and moss and mushrooms grew near streams, where peculiar and beautiful wildflowers bloomed on hillsides that never saw the sun. Unharmed, uncontaminated, not by choice, but by limitation.

It seemed like his world, and only his world. How easily and foolishly I forgot that other people inhabited the same acres.

Hands on hips, Adrian stopped in front of a flat stone. "It's a pioneer grave."

It looked like a rock to me. We both crouched and touched it. It was hot from the sun.

"When I was little, you could still read the name and date." Adrian ran his hand across the surface. "The grave belongs to a teenage girl."

"I wonder how she died."

"Diphtheria." He straightened. "That's what somebody said anyway. I've heard if you dig up the body, the disease will still be there. You can catch it."

I moved my hand away.

I didn't believe him, and now I began to wonder if it was really a grave at all. Just a flat stone. There were a lot of flat stones around. Or maybe the story was something he'd been told as a kid by an adult who was just messing with him.

I suddenly imagined the surface of the ground like the soft leathery covering that protected a walnut, hiding a secret world just under our feet. Not compact, but a network of tunnels and caves and even streams. And the pioneer girl, dressed in an apron and bonnet. I imagined her with plump flesh and healthy skin, and I had to remind myself that if she was under there, she would be a skeleton. Just bones and rotten calico.

"So the guy who owns the bar is your uncle?" Adrian asked. "What about the rest of your family?"

I got to my feet and moved away from the grave. "My uncle and grandmother are the people I'm closest to."

"Father? Mother?"

"My parents divorced when I was little. My mother remarried and has a new life with her new husband. She cut off ties with her older children, and we never hear from her." The words came quickly, almost breathlessly. "She associates us with him. That's what it is. She can't look at us without being reminded of her first husband."

I didn't like to talk about my mother or father. It was embarrassing. I tried to tell myself that I had nothing to be ashamed of, but when you're abandoned by both parents, it's hard not to feel that you did something wrong. Hard not to feel flawed and damaged.

"If you were to meet her, you'd think she was charming for about an hour, or a day, or maybe even a week. But she's not a nice person."

I suppose her bitterness toward life was understandable. How could a beautiful young woman not crack after being left for a wealthy divorcée old enough to be a grandmother? "My older brother is married and dealing with issues of his own," I said. "My younger brother is part of my mother's new family. I rarely hear from either of them."

I could see Adrian found my history and lack of family ties a curiosity. "What about you?" I asked.

He'd fallen into step beside me. "I have a sister and brother, but they don't have anything to do with the farm. It's just me, my father, and my mother."

"But your family has farmed the same ground for a long time, right?"

"I'm the fifth generation."

"It would be nice to have such deep roots." An alien concept for me, someone who'd never stayed in one place very long. Someone who never even thought about the future. Someone with the life expectancy of a mayfly.

"So you want kids?" he asked.

The thought of me as a mom was absurd. But why not? Creating my own family. "Yeah." And anyway, that kind of thing lurked in the future, and the future didn't exist for me.

"How many?"

"How many?" I laughed. "I don't know. Two? Three?" What did it matter? Not when today was one of those gorgeous spring days that came before the oppressive heat of summer. Brilliant blue sky, and air so dry the shadows were almost black.

For me our hike was random, but it had to be different for Adrian since he knew where he was going and what lay beyond each twist and turn.

At one point, I caught a glimpse of what looked like a small structure through a cluster of trees. I picked up my pace, lifting my knees and raising my arms so thorns and branches wouldn't scratch me.

Adrian hurried after me and grabbed my hand, trying to tug me in the opposite direction. "This way."

"I think I saw a building."

"There are a few old settler cabins around. Nothing interesting."

"I want to see." I slipped away from him and ran through the woods.

Yes, a cabin. The windows and doors were covered with plywood. Vines crept across the porch and roof, vanishing into cracks. I put my palm against the plywood door as if feeling for signs of life. "You should fix this up."

"The shed was built for my great-grandmother when she had tuberculosis." The words came out like a confession. "They thought the fresh air would do her good, but they also wanted to keep her away from her kids so they wouldn't catch it. She died when she was really young. In her twenties, I think."

"Oh." Deep roots also meant you were surrounded by reminders of lives cut short. Lots of lives, lots of deaths. "I'm sorry."

"It happened before I was born, but I don't like the place."

He hung back, as if he couldn't make himself step any closer. "Some people say the farm is cursed."

"That's ridiculous," I said.

"Is it?"

"Don't tell me you believe in that kind of thing."

He shrugged, lit a cigarette, and leaned against the trunk of a tree, arms and ankles crossed. "A lot of people have died on this farm."

I eyed a wasp nest in a corner of the porch, and I rubbed my arms even though I wasn't cold. "Farming is a dangerous occupation."

"Some of the deaths had nothing to do with farming. Like the kids my grandparents lost. Carbon monoxide poisoning. A freak accident. And the guy who hung himself..." He shook his head.

"So you think there's a curse?"

"Not an actual spell or anything like that, but some kind of massively bad mojo. If we're talking about that kind of thing, then yeah, I think the place is cursed." He was smoking like mad now, and I could tell the topic was making him nervous. He offered me a drag, and I shook my head.

The hand with the cigarette trembled. "I could tell you stories about this place, but I won't."

I didn't know what to make of him. Someone who came across as tough and incredibly masculine, now suddenly displaying an irrational side. But then I've never understood the fear some people have of black cats and the number thirteen.

A color. A number. These things have no control over us. But who was I to attempt to trivialize his very real emotions? Fear was real, even when the trigger was nothing more than superstitious nonsense.

"So do you believe in ghosts?" I immediately regretted my question; I could see the direction of the conversation was making him increasingly uncomfortable, and for a fraction of a second he seemed as fearful as a child.

"I've seen things," he said. "When I'm plowing the fields late at night. Things I can't explain."

"Darkness can play tricks on you."

Adrian gave himself a shake, as if throwing off something invisible. "Come on." He laughed in an obvious attempt to make me think he'd been kidding about ghosts and curses. And maybe he had. "We shouldn't be talking about this depressing stuff. We shouldn't be talking about sad things. Let's keep walking. I want to show you the apple trees."

CHAPTER FIVE

Fifteen minutes later, Adrian and I came upon a small grouping of apple trees hardly bigger than twigs.

"They're straight from every angle," I said, amazed.

"It's called checking. The trees are lined up with string. It's kind of a lost art since most people don't plant orchards by hand anymore." He bent to examine a sapling, then straightened. "Do you know you could sow every seed from every apple on a single tree and you wouldn't get the original variety? In fact, no two seeds would grow the same tree."

"Why's that?"

"Apple seeds don't contain genetic DNA."

"Would you get something better?"

"One in a million chance. Most likely all the seedlings would be inferior to the original."

I imagined an orchard where no two trees were alike. Each tree would have a different name, a new name.

"These saplings were all grafted," he said. "It's the only way to end up with marketable apples."

I could see the misshapen bump low on the trunk where the two varieties had been forced into something they weren't meant to be. So strange to think the rootstock was a completely different creature from the rest of the tree. Cutting and binding two living things together until they became one.

"One day I was trimming and noticed that a single branch on one of the heirlooms was different from the rest of the tree," Adrian told me. "A mutation called a bud sport. I flagged it, and when fall came I discovered that the apples on that single branch were some of the best I'd ever eaten. The original tree was destroyed by lightning, but luckily I'd grafted scions from the branch, and this is the result."

"Do the new trees have a name?"

"Sweet Melinda."

"Melinda...That's lovely."

I wondered whom he'd once known named Melinda. The girl he'd almost married?

Jealousy was a foreign emotion, and I had to look away. I thought about what Larry had said. What the psychic had told the police. A body hidden in a grove of trees. "I've heard that apple seeds are poisonous. Is that true?"

"Apple seeds contain a small amount of cyanide." Was that annoyance in his voice?

"I wonder how many seeds it would take to kill a person."

"A lot."

"Hundreds? Thousands?"

"I don't know. A cup, maybe. I've eaten a lot of apple seeds in my life and have never gotten sick."

In another section of the orchard, we approached a tree that had a small red box hanging from a branch. Adrian tipped the container and looked inside, then reached into the pocket of his flannel shirt and pulled out a notepad. "We're monitoring for codling moths." He uncapped a pen and jotted something down. "The traps contain pheromones that attract the moth. We check them every three days and make a record of how many codling moths we find. That determines what and when to spray." He returned the pad and pen to his pocket.

We sat down in the shade of one of the older, larger apple trees.

He looked me in the eye and said, "I like to draw." It was a bold declaration, or possibly a confession. Farmers didn't draw. "Usually with pencil," he said, "but also with pen and ink."

It wasn't the tone of his confession that struck me but the admission itself. I drew. And pen and ink was my favorite medium. "I draw too," I told him. "Also in pen and ink." I had a portfolio and tablets full of my drawings, and I dreamed of going to art school.

Adrian was looking at me as if he couldn't believe it. "I've never known anyone else who uses pen and ink," he said with excitement. In a fraction of a second, we'd gone from having nothing in common to being two artistic oddballs who'd somehow found each other.

"What kinds of things do you draw?" I asked.

"Animals. Plants. People." He pulled out the pen again...and he drew on me in black ink. I watched him sketch a morning glory, then a thistle. Even on skin, his drawings were accurate.

"They're all weeds." I turned my arm, admiring his skill. "Bane of a farmer's existence. Draw something you don't need to eradicate."

His brows met as he gave it some thought; then he began drawing again.

He smelled like hay and apple cider. And if beneath that he also smelled like pulpy roots and the garlic odor of the farmers who visited the bar, I chose to ignore it.

"An apple?" That was kind of obvious.

"Not any apple."

"Oh?"

"This apple is a Red Delicious."

"How can you tell?"

"It's tall and narrow and has bumps on the bottom."

"Is it sour? I like sour apples."

"It's sweet. An eating apple. Almost too sweet."

"So it's something else you don't like?"

The edge of his mouth curled in amusement. "I don't like Red Delicious apples. But they're more aesthetically pleasing than say... Jonathans. Red Delicious have nicer skin. Flawless, less prone to scab. Red Delicious can actually look purple if temperatures drop the right number of degrees at just the right time. They're beautiful."

"Well, I'm glad you didn't draw a damaged apple. An apple with a hole in it."

"Do you know what makes that hole? The codling moth worm. Once the codling moth takes over an orchard, the trees can't be saved. It takes a lot of pesticide to create a beautiful, perfect apple."

"What does a codling moth look like?"

"Like this."

He drew it on my inner arm, the white flesh just below the elbow. There was something mysterious about the lines of the moth. Something that felt old and timeless. "I once read a book that said moths were really souls," I told him.

The moth looked sinister, and now it was on my skin. I imagined going back to the bar and trying to scrub it off. It made me feel the way reading the mushroom book had made me feel, filling me with an inexplicable dread. As if the image itself were somehow leaching poison into my skin.

Death will occur within hours.

"What's wrong? Don't you like my moth?"

"It's something else you work to eradicate."

"You asked me about it."

"I know, but…" I looked at it again.

Why, it was beautiful, with dark patterns on delicately fringed wings. What had I been thinking? But it had seemed sinister a moment earlier. Sometimes sensations come over me that have nothing to do with reality.

Adrian bent his head, and I could smell his hair, and beyond that I could smell the scent of chemicals.

The wind kicked up, shaking the fescue and stirring the wildflowers, sending pollen in our direction. From far away came the familiar background noise of a farmer driving a tractor across a field.

"Give me the pen," I said. "I want to write you a note." He made me feel more feminine than I'd ever felt in my life. If I didn't watch out, I'd soon be polishing my nails and wearing perfume.

I pulled his arm to my lap and pushed up his sleeve. I could see the pores. I could see the blond hair on his tan arms. I could feel the sinewy muscles and veins beneath the skin. Farming had made him hard and strong.

"What are you going to write?"

"You'll see."

Dear Adrian.

He twisted for a better view.

"Don't look." I shielded his arm so he couldn't see.

I thought about writing *love me* but restrained myself.

I was certain that years later I would recall the texture and taste of the day. I would remember the sun on my face, the smell of grass and earth, the distilled brilliance of the sky. My capacity for sensation was in the red zone. Life magnified, as if the day had been built just for me.

Be mine, I wrote on his arm. A harmless thing to say. A Valentine-candy sentiment. But he had to be mine. He could belong to no one else.

He touched the faint red mark on my wrist. "How did this happen?"

I shrugged and pulled away. He pulled me back.

"Kids do stupid things," I said.

"How old were you?"

"Fourteen."

"I'm glad you're still here." He traced a finger over the red line before lifting my wrist to his lips. Then he slipped the pen from my fingers and proceeded to draw a bracelet on my arm. A beautiful thing of vines and leaves. Making it all better.

Once or twice I wondered what time it was. I'd told my uncle I would be back by four, but I didn't care. I never wanted to leave. I didn't want the day to end.

Later, when we finally headed to the bar, I came upon a sketch pad tucked behind a toolbox on the passenger floor of Adrian's truck. I opened it and discovered several pencil sketches of a girl who looked familiar. Some were faces, and some were full bodies.

"Is this me?" I asked, even though I knew it was.

He glanced away from the road, let out a curse, and snatched the sketchbook from my hand. "Don't look at that." He slowed the truck long enough to tuck the drawings behind the seat. His face was red.

The few drawings I'd seen represented hours of work. I touched the side of my face and imagined a charcoal tip moving across textured paper.

I suppose infatuation and crushes start in a flash. Two days ago, he didn't know I existed. Now he was spending hours drawing pictures of me, and I was already dreading the hours we would be apart. This was all the harder for me to grasp because I'd never understood how girls got wrapped up in guys. That wasn't me. I prided myself on remaining true to who I was. I prided myself on needing no one. I'd watched women fade to become someone else. To become more like their boyfriends, taking on their likes and dislikes. Dressing differently. Talking differently. Giving up who they were. I was suddenly one of those girls. Lovesick. Helpless. Weak. Overpowered by something beyond my control.

Lovesickness can't be explained in any rational way.

He was just a man. Arms and legs, skin and hair. Just a man. Nothing special about him. And yet there was. Something very special. Something that spoke to me and only me.

I observed my obsession with a distant part of my mind, my only fear being that this might end too soon. Maybe today. Maybe tomorrow.

I couldn't imagine never seeing him again or never experiencing another afternoon like the afternoon we'd just shared.

I may have been infatuated with Adrian, but he seemed to be equally infatuated with me. He showed up at the bar, pretending I wasn't the reason behind his visits, sometimes not even engaging in conversation until hours had passed. Then he began stopping in at closing time, and he would casually invite me to join him, as if the idea had just entered his head. I found his behavior enchanting, because I wasn't the kind of girl to be courted in a traditional way.

In the dark, in the middle of the night, he and I would sit by the river, or sit by the pond, or sit in the pasture in front of a bonfire. Early evenings, when it was still light, we took sketch pads to the orchard and lounged under trees. Adrian admired my skill, but he was a much better artist than I was, and he had a distinctive style, something I hadn't yet developed. If I were to line up my pen and ink, the work would appear to have been drawn by twenty different people, but Adrian had a unique and recognizable approach, especially in his depiction of horses in motion.

Sometimes on our outings I packed a picnic, and sometimes we ended up in a canoe on the pond. It was always spontaneous, whatever we felt like doing at the moment, and it was romantic in all the ways I would expect something to be romantic, designed just for us, our days and evenings of nature and art. Some might say it wasn't healthy for two people to spend every moment alone together, but if others had been around we would have ignored them. We wouldn't have given them a second thought.

CHAPTER SIX

"How about a game of pool?" my uncle asked.

The bar was empty, and we often shot pool to pass the time.

I racked up the balls and he broke, dropping a solid green seven but missing the red three.

"I'm worried about you," he said.

I knew he was talking about the amount of time I was spending with Adrian. "He's a good guy," I told him.

"You haven't known him long enough to know who he is. He's not like us. He's not like you."

"Is hanging out with him any worse than what I'm doing now?"

I had stripes. I didn't like stripes. I chalked my stick and took aim at the nine ball.

The game was a choreographed dance. Left hand reaches for the square of blue; chalk the tip while eying the table. Look ahead to predict where the upcoming play will end and the next begin. It was all about setting up the next shot. If you're really good, setting up several shots.

"Living in a bar?" I dropped three balls then missed a bank.

"You never seemed to mind when you needed a place to crash."

He moved methodically, slowly, without pause. He was an engineer, so angles came naturally to him, and yet my uncle missed an easy shot. Not only missed, but scratched.

I thought about the moss that grew in his toilet. It was several inches long and undulated like kelp. Whenever I used his shower, I always did so with the intention of not looking in the toilet. But I could never help myself. I had to lift the lid. And the moss was always there. I sometimes imagined goldfish happily swimming between the gently moving strands, bright orange against dark green.

This hadn't always been my uncle's life. At one time he'd lived in Chicago, where he'd worn suits and white collars. Where he'd lived in a penthouse overlooking the Magnificent Mile and a maid had come to clean once a week.

But things happen. He'd given a friend a ride across the country only to discover that the friend had murdered someone the night before. The next thing you know, my uncle was a felon who no longer had a need for suits and white collars. He was here because he had nowhere else to go.

I think my uncle wanted to share his misery with me. Who would peel pickled eggs with him while he listened to Paul Harvey? Who would take his coupons to the grocery store and buy forty frozen pizzas for a buck each?

We were an odd couple, and he would miss me if I left.

But I was already gone.

He knew it. I was sure he knew it.

Even now I was thinking of the way Adrian's skin felt under my fingers, and if I turned my head quickly enough, I swear I could smell him in my hair.

Uncle Jim knew I sometimes didn't come home until dawn. When I finally returned, I would sneak into the bar, grabbing the door chimes so they wouldn't ring, so he wouldn't hear them through the intercom system in his trailer. But he always knew.

"You can't get mixed up with him." Faded blue eyes looked at me from across green felt. An Elton John song played on the jukebox. A song I'd never liked. Elton could do better than that.

When I was four, my uncle had taken me to a zoo where we saw a baby polar bear playing with a beach ball. The animal was full of crazy joy. People crowded around, watching and laughing. I giggled so hard I almost wet my pants. We returned to the zoo a year later. I couldn't wait to see the polar bear again, but when we got there he just sat and stared into space.

"What's wrong with him?" I'd asked.

"He's grown up now," my uncle had replied.

The grief I felt that day was a grief of the marrow. I'd grieved for the bear, and I'd grieved for life, and I'd grieved for myself and for the uncle holding my hand. Because in my child's heart, I knew the bear had finally realized the cage was his life.

"I don't want to see you hurt," my uncle now told me. A nice way of saying Adrian would dump me when he got bored. Maybe he was right. I'd seen it happen all my life, so it was something I'd considered, and the thought made my stomach twist until it felt like I was bleeding inside.

My uncle's disapproval made me want Adrian more.

Without conscious thought, I put into play lessons Uncle Jim had taught me. "Eight ball in the side pocket." I took aim. Low, snap, click, recoil. The smudged white ball jumped back to where it had started, and the black eight dropped neatly and solidly. A good sound.

"You don't know anything about him." And then my uncle, who'd never in his life given me a direct order, said, "I think you should stay away from him. You should stop seeing Adrian Curtis."

CHAPTER SEVEN

"I'm going to have to move." I passed the bottle of wine to Adrian. We were lying on a quilt a few feet from the edge of a pond, stars overhead, clouds, a half-moon. Crickets and frogs and fireflies. Another beautiful night together.

Of course, *move* for me simply meant pack my car. I could have it loaded in fifteen minutes.

"Move?" He took a swallow of wine. "Why?"

"My uncle and I aren't getting along." I couldn't take it anymore. The cold silence. The looks of disapproval from someone who'd always adored me.

"What's wrong?"

Why had I started this? It would ruin our time together. I lit a cigarette and tossed the pack on the blanket. "He doesn't think you and I should see each other. It's nothing personal. He just..." My words trailed off. Saying my uncle didn't want me to get hurt implied that Adrian and I had a relationship.

"You wouldn't move far, would you?"

Did I detect a hint of panic in his voice? "I don't know."

There were no towns between my uncle's bar and Adrian's farm. I'd have to go in the other direction, across the river into Iowa. Maybe I could find a cheap apartment there. Maybe I could get a job tending bar, a job that actually paid money. Right now I was making room and board. A sofa bed and all the Stewart's sandwiches and pickled eggs I could eat. How could a gal leave that behind?

"All I know is that I can't deal with him any longer." I'd endured one hostile adult for too many years. I didn't need another.

"Come live with me."

Had I heard right? I had a buzz going, and maybe the roar in my head had distorted his words.

"There's a house on the farm that's supposed to be for me." He took a drag from his cigarette. The tip glowed, and I could briefly see his face, his eyes squinted against the smoke. "It's tiny. Originally built for apple pickers."

Everything shifted.

What I had known as my life changed in a matter of seconds. Like finding out you'd put a puzzle together all wrong. I dumped the pieces and began reconstructing, creating a completely new picture.

Did he mean what he was saying, or was it something he wouldn't give any thought to, come morning?

I didn't want him to think this was what I'd been angling for, because it wasn't. "Move in together...Wow. I don't know..." My response was cautious with a touch of disinterest.

"Not move in together. Get married. We'd have to get married."

If we hadn't been the only two people there, I would have looked over my shoulder to see if he was talking to someone else. Married. We'd barely just met. "You're drunk." I held my breath.

"Not *that* drunk."

"Married..." Moving in together, yes. But marriage...A legal commitment. I had serious doubts.

"We hardly know each other."

"Some people are together for years, and they've never really known each other. We know each other as well as a lot of people do."

True.

"I'm going about this all wrong. It should have been dinner and a ring."

"I don't like rings."

"Well, dinner."

"I'm a nonconformist. I wouldn't have liked that either."

He laughed but quickly became serious again. "Say yes."

I took one drag followed by another. The hot cigarette burned my throat. "When? How?"

"As soon as possible."

This was crazy. This was insane. I'd been wondering how I would ever live without him once he quit coming around, and now he was asking me to marry him.

It would never happen. That's what I told myself.

I was old enough to know that life was full of disappointments and the things you want most are usually unattainable. But for right now, for tonight, I would savor the thought of our spending the rest of our lives together, even if it didn't happen, even if he changed his mind in the morning. Even if he acted as if this conversation had never taken place.

A sound penetrated the buzz in my head. Something external. Something far away in the night. "What's that?" I asked.

"I don't hear anything."

"A motor or something."

"Oh, *that*. The orchard sprayer. I didn't even notice. Guess I'm used to it."

"Now?" It had to be two or three o'clock in the morning.

"My father likes to spray the apples at night. Less drift, and the sun doesn't evaporate the pesticide. Gives it more of a chance to work."

The sound of the sprayer faded, then returned.

Hypnotic, methodic, repetitious.

I imagined tractor and sprayer moving between the rows of trees, a cloud of chemicals coating leaves and small, developing apples.

When it reached the end of the row, the motor shut down, and the tractor circled and lined up for the return. The whir began again. The sound of the sprayer blended oddly with the sounds of the frogs and crickets, reminding me of the story of Lily.

"Have you ever seen anyone drink farm chemicals?" I asked.

"I saw a salesman drink herbicide." Adrian was obviously uncomfortable, and I could tell he wondered if he should have admitted to such a thing. At the same time, his voice held unease, the same unease I'd heard that day in the woods, by the old cabin. Adrian was telling me he'd seen someone drink farm chemicals. It was the closest I'd ever come to finding Lily, whether she truly existed or not.

"Did the salesman have a little girl with him? A girl named Lily?"

"I've heard that story too."

"Is it true?"

"It's just a legend," Adrian said.

"But you saw a man drink herbicide?"

"It was common practice at one time. I saw several men drink it."

I imagined a group of grown men standing around, laughing, lifting glasses, and cheering one another. "Did you ever drink herbicide?"

"God, no."

His denial of ever having participated in something so foolish should have reassured me, but it didn't. And now I finally had proof that the story about the girl was at least half true.

CHAPTER EIGHT

Adrian didn't forget. The next day, he was more insistent than ever. Through a haze of bewilderment and disbelief, I went with him to get a marriage license.

Maybe it would really happen.

That night as we closed the bar, I told my uncle about the upcoming nuptials. I thought he'd see that he'd been wrong, see that I was more to Adrian than someone he would eventually toss away.

"You barely know him."

My own words coming back at me, but now I found them irritating and misplaced. I had proof that my uncle had been wrong about Adrian's feelings toward me, but he still wasn't accepting the relationship.

He draws flowers on my arms. He wants me to marry him. "Can't you believe he cares about me?"

"That's not what concerns me. My God. Just stop and use your head for a minute. Give it a few more months. If you both really care for each other, a few months won't make any difference."

But everything had already been set in motion, and I'd already mentally moved away from those long hours when Adrian wasn't in my life. Now that the idea of marriage had been planted in my brain, I couldn't go back. It was so close; I could almost see myself wearing an apron and shirtwaist dress, taking a roast from the oven. And my uncle had unwittingly played a role. He'd driven me away. I felt a certain satisfaction in that. *See what you did?* I wanted to point this out to him, but surely he knew. Surely he could see that his disapproval had set me upon this new path.

"When everybody said you knowingly gave a murderer a ride across the country, I didn't believe them," I said. "I defended you. I told people you were innocent."

"That's different."

"It's not."

"He's practically a stranger to you. You know nothing about him."

I started thinking about the day-to-day of what marrying Adrian meant. About moving out. No more sofa bed. No more sleeping with my head just feet from the men's urinal. No more sneaking back in the middle of the night. No more Stewart's sandwiches.

I looked up at the dust-covered Avon bottles behind the bar and felt a brief twinge. My uncle would be alone. He would listen to Paul Harvey and peel eggs by himself. I'd been told that if eggs remained in vinegar long enough, you could bounce them. I'd never tried it. I'd always wanted to try it.

Adrian.

The sorrow I felt floated away as quickly as it had come. Adrian. Twenty-four hours a day. My head almost exploded with the euphoria of it. Two days ago, I would have thought it impossible. I wouldn't have believed it.

"Are you sure you understood him correctly?"

Maybe Uncle Jim and my mother were more alike than I'd thought. "You're mean."

"It's just... I'm not saying he can't love you, but..."

Why couldn't he just be happy for me? "God forbid I end up with a felon who sells porn." The words just popped out, but I didn't regret them. He was hurting me; I wanted to hurt him back.

"You've been on a path of self-destruction your whole life," my uncle said. "Adrian is just another mistake. A big one."

He was wrong. "I'm breaking a pattern. Can't you see that?" Oh, what was the point? He would never understand.

It was over. I could kiss this dark life good-bye. A new life was ahead of me. A perfect life.

My uncle was jealous. And maybe there was even more to his reaction than jealousy. Who else would work for him? Nobody.

"You don't want me to leave. You don't want to lose your free labor." I didn't have much of a temper, but I was getting mad. I almost said he didn't want to die alone in the middle of nowhere, but I stopped myself. Because it held too much truth, and I couldn't be *that* cruel. But I wouldn't let him spoil my happiness. I wouldn't let him make me feel guilty.

"Go ahead, then. Marry your farmer. Your cursed golden boy. And when you come to your senses, don't come back here. Don't come knocking on my door in the middle of the night begging me to give you a job and a place to sleep."

CHAPTER NINE

The next morning, long before the bar opened, I loaded my battered white Mustang with all of my belongings. Boxes of books, sketch pads, ink and pens, journals, two acoustic guitars, three boxes of albums, and an old Remington typewriter in a black, pressed-cardboard case covered in something meant to look like leather. The few clothes I owned, purchased mostly from thrift shops, fit in a mint green suitcase with silver hinges and snap locks that were known to pop open.

Once I had the car packed, I ate my last fake sandwich, then I locked the front door, removed the key from my key ring, and slipped it through the mail slot.

I didn't tell my uncle good-bye. I might feel bad about that later, but not now. Now it felt right.

I drove to Adrian's farm, turning off the highway onto a blacktop road that led south. Three miles and the peak of the farmhouse roof appeared. Behind the house was a circular drive that opened to a white barn and sheds.

It felt strange to come here without Adrian, like a different place.

I cut the engine and stepped from the car, remaining in the V of the open door, one foot inside. The house had two porches with ornate trim, an American flag, hanging pink petunias, windows of stained glass.

A curtain dropped, a door slammed, and a middle-aged woman came down the walk toward me. She was gingham, dark curly hair, rosy cheeks, Keds. A magazine-ad mom, alien yet familiar. I knew it was Adrian's mother. I even knew that her name was Ruth. I'd bought cider from her in the salesroom, but I doubted she'd remember me—just one of hundreds of customers stopping on a busy fall day.

"Are you here for apples?" Her voice was a friendly singsong. "Apple season won't start for another three months. We'll have some Transparents before that, but I already have more orders than I can fill." Behind her, bees buzzed in the spirea bushes.

"I'm looking for Adrian."

She frowned and dropped the friendly face. "He's working."

I told her my name, hoping to clarify things.

She glanced at my car, loaded with boxes and clothes. "Looks like you're moving."

"Is Adrian around?"

Her expression became even more remote. "Adrian works all day. He's in the field right now and won't be done until after dark."

"I didn't know you raised crops too."

"We have crops and cattle, but what business is it of yours?"

Her open hostility took me by surprise. "If you tell me where he is, I'll find him myself."

"I said he's busy." She made a shooing motion with her hands.

"Adrian hasn't mentioned me?" I asked.

"Oh, he's mentioned you."

What did that mean? "Did he tell you we're getting married?"

"Adrian is too young. He has a long time to think about finding a wife and having a family."

I was beginning to feel a familiar sick dread. Had Adrian changed his mind? Had he even meant to marry me in the first place?

"He's only twenty-three," she said. "How old are you? You don't look a day over sixteen."

"I'm twenty-one." No need to mention that I hadn't been twenty-one very long. Funny that she thought twenty-three was young. It seemed old to me.

She straightened, making herself taller. "You'll just get bored," she predicted. "Get bored and move on to someone else." She crossed her arms and fixed me with a hard stare. I doubt I was the first girlfriend to be chased off.

But instead of leaving the farm, I headed down a gravel road, past the orchard, where I spotted a red tractor pulling a yellow sprayer through a cornfield. I parked my car in the shallow ditch, got out, and waited for the driver to complete his journey across the field.

I waved.

He saw me, drove the tractor to the gate, shut it down, and jumped to the ground.

Adrian. Dressed in jeans, a leather belt, boots, and a dark T-shirt. His arms were covered with a fine layer of dirt. Even his eyelashes were dusted. He tapped out a filterless cigarette, popped it in his mouth, and lit it. "I thought I was picking you up at the bar later."

I told him about my uncle, and I told him about the encounter with his mother. This was where he'd confess that he'd changed his mind.

"I ignore her as much as possible." He shrugged. "She goes her way and I go mine."

Now I thought I understood why he was intrigued by my lack of family ties. Unlike me, he couldn't just pack and leave when things became unbearable. My entire life had been about moving, leaving. Had his mother accidentally tapped into an inherent part of my personality? And was she simply looking out for her son?

"Don't worry," Adrian said. "She'll eventually come around."

I had doubts about that, but I wasn't sure I even cared. I was marrying Adrian, not her.

I created a space for him in the car. He wedged himself into the passenger seat, a crate of my junk on his lap. Uncomfortable, but we didn't have far to go.

I made a three-point turn and headed back the way I'd come, toward the farmhouse. Following Adrian's directions, I drove past a grove of apple trees and a pond to finally reach a grass-and-gravel lane that ended at a small white dwelling, set back from the road but still close to the main house. Cement steps led to a cement stoop.

"It was originally built by settlers, then updated over the years for pickers," Adrian explained. "Has some of the original hand-hewn logs and floor. Very rustic, I'm warning you."

We unloaded my car, piling everything against one wall in the living room.

The cramped, two-bedroom structure smelled stale, like a building that no one had lived in for a long time; obviously Adrian came here only occasionally. It was furnished with a double bed and sofa. A wood-burning stove stood in one corner. The only source of heat? For someone who'd been living in a bar, it seemed pretty nice. My own space. Our space.

"It needs a little work," Adrian admitted.

I could already imagine some of the things I would do. Fresh paint. A small table in the kitchen with flowers in the center.

Married.

He reached for me, pulling me close. I caught the heavy, pungent scent of chemicals. As soon as I touched him, I tasted garlic on my tongue. "Haven't you been spraying?"

"I've been around pesticides and herbicides my whole life, and I'm healthy."

He *was* the picture of health. I couldn't deny that.

We shed our clothes and tumbled to the mattress. A bed. Another first. Somehow a bed seemed *too* normal. A bed seemed wrong.

I wondered if he'd brought other girls here. I tried not to think about that.

His skin felt fevered and hot from the sun. Sweat dripped from his hair and fell on my face. It ran into my mouth, tasting like salt and dirt and the spray from the field—already a taste and smell I associated with him.

CHAPTER TEN

The next day, my paternal grandmother and I stood side by side in the tiny kitchen of her Burlington, Iowa, home, both of us wrapped in floral-print aprons as we crushed strawberries, the bouquet of lilacs behind the sink filling the room with a scent I loved even though it was cloying. Canning jars and lids had been sterilized and were lined up on the red Formica tabletop, the glass still hot from the high-temperature bath.

With stained wooden spoons, my grandmother and I poured and scooped the strawberries into a deep pan on the stove. She lit the gas burner, adjusted the flame, and shook out the match, leaving a puff of sulfur behind. Ever since the day the city gas had gone crazy and pilot lights shot three feet high, my grandmother had used matches. No more pilot lights for her.

While she stirred, I added lemon juice and pectin to the fruit.

I nervously rubbed one bare foot over the other. "I've met somebody," I told her.

She adjusted the flour-sack towel on her shoulder. "I figured something was going on. Hadn't seen you around much."

"We're going to get married."

She didn't even look up, and there was no hesitation in the hand that stirred the strawberries. "Hmm."

"Soon. Really soon."

"Hmm."

Maybe it was a German thing, but my grandmother had never once hugged or kissed me. I didn't care. I wasn't a hugger either, and I knew she loved me deeply. Through her, I kept up on my father's life, and sometimes he and I even crossed paths, usually by accident.

"What about your art?" she asked. "What about school?"

She'd been a clerk in the men's department of JCPenney most of her married life, but her first paying job had been guitar accompaniment to silent movies, and I'd grown up listening to her play and sing. She understood the heart of an artist. As she'd aged, her voice had gotten horrible, but that didn't stop her from a weekly round of tunes.

"I'll keep drawing," I said. But I had to wonder if I'd ever make it to art school. "Adrian is an artist too. Pen and ink, just like me."

"Does he like strawberry jam?" she asked. "This beau of yours?"

"I don't know."

"What kind of food *does* he like?"

He liked beer. He liked wine. "I have no idea."

Both of her heavily painted eyebrows shot up. Her thoughts needed no words. "Bring him over and I'll fix him some of my potato pancakes."

I suppose it was a bad sign, but it was impossible to imagine Adrian in her house, sitting at her table, eating her pancakes.

When I told her who he was, I could see her struggling to put her own emotions and concerns in the proper place. On one hand, you don't marry someone you hardly know; on the other, he wasn't some unemployed alcoholic who'd stumbled into my uncle's bar. Adrian came from good stock. Solid stock. To her mind, he was someone who could take care of me, give me a home, a stable life. None of those things mattered to me, but I knew that's what she was thinking. She'd worried about me for years, and now that she was a retired widow, I'm sure she wanted someone else to take over.

"If you live on a farm, he's going to expect you to cook for him. Three hot meals a day. Is that what you want? Cooking for a man? Cleaning up after a man?"

"I can do it."

She looked skeptical. "He won't be satisfied with that granola you like to make, or those tomato sandwiches you're always eating."

I laughed just thinking about presenting him with either of those things.

"Here." She leaned the spoon in my direction.

I took over stirring while she lit a menthol cigarette. Then she was back, squinting her eyes against the smoke as she tapped the spoon on the side of the pan and tamped down the flame. "I suppose I could teach you how to cook a few things. Find out what he likes, and I'll put some recipes together."

I'd lived with my grandmother off and on, but my late nights and an undependable car made it easier to stay at my uncle's. But I visited her when I could. Many times I'd watched her do her domestic chores with a cigarette bobbing from the corner of her mouth the way it was now. Hanging clothes on the line, ironing, cooking. The cigarette was always there. I could feel the smashed pack in the back pocket of my cutoffs, and I briefly thought of joining her for a smoke, but I hadn't yet reached the point where I could puff away while engaged in another activity.

"That would be great," I said, while at the same time imagining my grandmother's goulash and creamed corn. White bread with a slab of cold butter topped with grape jelly. Or worse, her sauerkraut and hot dogs. Somehow I didn't think those kinds of meals would appeal to Adrian either. But I could make tacos. I could make pizza.

"Farming is a hard life," she said.

She'd grown up on a farm, moved to the city, and never looked back. But farm life had made her tough, and she could do anything a man could do, from shooting a rifle to building a house.

"Does he treat you right?"

I was relieved to see that she'd already accepted the inevitable. Unlike my uncle, she wouldn't get mad and wouldn't reject me.

"That's the main thing," she said. "Because if he doesn't, you don't have any business marrying him. I don't care how pretty he is, or how blue his eyes are, or how many acres his parents own, or how good he is in the sack."

"Grandma!"

"Well, it's true."

But she got me inside and out, and I'm sure she knew there was nothing she could say that would change my mind.

"Strawberries are boiling," she said. "You can add the sugar now."

The Marriage

CHAPTER ELEVEN

I would have preferred that our marriage take place at the county court-house, but Adrian couldn't turn his back on tradition and had confessed to wanting a ceremony in a church. It was supposed to be just the two of us. Inviting no one solved many problems considering the odd relationship I had with my mother, my absent father, the fight I'd had with my uncle, and no friends in the area since I hadn't lived there long. But at the last minute Ruth had insisted she and Adrian's father be present.

Her insistence upon coming was odd, especially after the way she'd treated me. The day was ruined. "Couldn't you just tell her no?" I'd asked.

"Nobody tells my mother no," Adrian had said. "She'd just come anyway."

My grandmother would have been hurt if she'd discovered she hadn't been invited, so she was present too. A few bodies in the front pew. I knew they were there, but it almost seemed they belonged to another dimension. My heart was beating too fast, and anything beyond me, Adrian, and the minister was a blur.

Standing at the altar, Adrian looked handsome in the black suit he'd worn the first time I'd seen him. I wore a cream-colored sweater and a long brown skirt with brown boots. My head was buzzing because of what we were about to do. I felt a sweaty, heightened euphoria. The kind of thing you get when a roller coaster is slowly approaching the peak.

The interior of the church smelled like furniture polish and old wood. In the subdued light, Adrian looked deathly pale, his face covered with a sheen of perspiration. Something of his terror transmitted to me.

Should we stop? But we were rolling, and I felt unable to speak up. You can't stop the ride once it starts.

I didn't want to examine the situation. I didn't want to think of the consequences of what I was doing, what we were doing. No negative thoughts were allowed. I knew if I started thinking about all the reasons we shouldn't do this, I would panic.

Outside, the wind picked up and the room darkened. A downpour followed, and the roar of the rain against the roof and windows drowned out the minister.

As soon as he pronounced us man and wife, Adrian's mother began to sob.

Then it was over.

The wedding and the rain.

Papers were signed and the minister was paid.

Outside, my grandmother tossed rice, laughing at her own cleverness, charmingly oblivious to the hostile undercurrents surrounding us.

Introductions were made, followed by brief, awkward conversation. An uncomfortable glance passed from mother, to father, to son, and in that moment I knew without a doubt that Ruth had tried to talk Adrian out of marriage. I had to wonder at the scene that must have taken place just hours earlier on the farm. Shouting? Begging? His mother trying to reason with him, pointing out the many ways a marriage to me was wrong and foolish? And what did he say in return? What did he tell her?

Regardless of the exact words, he'd apparently told her no.

A few stray raindrops fell from a blue sky. Adrian grabbed my arm, and we ran for the truck. A turn of the ignition key and we were on our way, heading for the farm over roads strewn with leaves and small branches. Steam rose from the blacktop, and the air smelled like rain-soaked earth.

"I need to check on the wind damage," Adrian said once we were in our little house.

I hadn't even thought of the trees. "Do you want me to come with you?"

"Stay here. I'll be back in about an hour."

While he was gone, I showered and changed into jeans and a T-shirt. I briefly thought about going to visit Adrian's mother, but that didn't seem like a good idea considering her behavior at the wedding.

The sky was beginning to darken, and Adrian still hadn't returned. I opened a couple of windows to let in fresh air. I smoked and waited.

Two more hours passed, and my annoyance turned to worry. I grabbed my car keys and hurried out the door. I had no idea where to begin looking, but I had to search.

I heard a truck and immediately recognized the distinctive sound of a diesel engine. And then Adrian was pulling up next to the cabin behind my car, shutting off the ignition while the vehicle continued to roll. The dome light briefly illuminated his face. He tumbled out the door, catching himself before he hit the ground.

"Where have you been? Are you okay?"

"Fine. I'm fine." His words were thick.

Drunk.

He shot for our little house, and I followed him inside, closing the door behind me. "You've been *drinking*?"

He dropped down on the couch and waved his hand. "A wedding celebration."

"Without me?"

"Just one drink."

"You've had more than one."

He tugged off his tie, then pushed himself to his feet and launched himself toward the bedroom, unbuttoning his shirt as he went. The shirt hit the floor and he fell across the mattress at the same time. "It was supposed to be just one, but people kept buying."

I untied his dress shoes, pulled them from his feet, and dropped them to the floor. He didn't budge.

I slipped out of my jeans and got into bed beside him. He was on top of the covers. I tugged, managing to free enough fabric to cover myself. "How were the trees?"

"Trees?"

"The *apple* trees. You went to check on the apple trees, remember?"

"A few small limbs broken, but that was it."

"Good."

He rolled to his back and put his arm over his eyes. "I feel sick."

"That's good too."

"I'm not used to drinking. Not serious drinking."

I turned off the bedside lamp. "You picked an odd day to go pro."

No answer.

A short time later his voice came out of the darkness, sad and forlorn. "Everybody's pissed off at me."

"Who? Your mother? Your father?"

He didn't answer my question, focusing instead on his line of thought. "What are we doing?" he said.

A few hours into his marriage and he was already experiencing regret. I didn't know if I should laugh or cry. I wanted to hit him, but I restrained myself. "Go to sleep," I told him.

"Maybe. If the room ever stops spinning."

What had I done? What had *we* done?

Same people.

Same world.

Yet nothing felt the same. *Nothing.*

The air had changed. The mood had changed. The color and shape, the texture and resonance of my life, had irrevocably changed. These were far-fetched and fanciful thoughts, because how could something change so drastically within a matter of a few hours?

But everything was different.

In that moment, I wondered if I should have listened to my uncle.

My car was outside. I could leave right now.

Where would I go? There was always my grandmother's house, but I didn't want to burden her, and she would have been so disappointed in me. No, I'd sleep on it. See if things were different tomorrow. See if they were better.

A few minutes later, Adrian began to snore.

CHAPTER TWELVE

Miami, Florida, and Burlington, Iowa, 1961

My parents divorced when I was six. One day my world was perfect; the next day my father sat down at the foot of my bed and told me I'd never see or hear from him again. We lived in Miami, Florida, and he was in charge of a deep-sea fishing boat, working for a divorcée who'd once been married to the prime minister of the Bahamas. She was twenty years older, enjoying a lavish lifestyle my father, in his early thirties, had only dreamed of. She lived in a mansion, had servants, a Rolls-Royce, and a swimming pool. He traded us for her.

The wounded always return home, and shortly after the divorce and two weeks after my mother gave birth to my younger brother, Uncle Jim paid for airline tickets and picked us up at Chicago O'Hare. His downtown apartment was unlike anything my young eyes had ever seen. Spotless, with shiny black surfaces and polished glass that displayed pieces of art. The closet in his bedroom was full of white dress shirts, dark slacks, and leather shoes lined up in a neat row. I inhaled the scent of clean, ironed shirts and aftershave.

He gave my mother his bed, and he slept on the foldout couch while my older brother and I took the floor. My new baby brother was put in a drawer that had been removed from a dresser.

Two days later, Uncle Jim drove us to Burlington, Iowa. My mother insisted we go past the house she and my father had once shared. A house he'd built shortly after their honeymoon.

"We were living there when you were born," my mother said from the passenger seat, baby in her arms, my uncle at the wheel. "Do you remember it?"

I shook my head. Nope. But I had one memory of sitting on the curb eating wet dirt with a spoon. I'd expected it to taste like chocolate pudding. I wasn't going to tell her about that.

The road ended in a circle, and my uncle turned the car around and we made another pass. We all stared out the window.

"I liked that house," my brother said.

Our mother sighed. "We should never have moved to Florida." She sounded so sad.

For a brief time, our life seemed to correct and stabilize. My mother got a job teaching at a Catholic school even though she'd only briefly attended a community college. Every weekday morning a sitter came to our apartment to take care of the baby while the rest of us packed into the car and headed for school. I wore a blue plaid jumper with white kneesocks, my brother a white shirt and navy blue slacks. Our mother dressed in a stylish skirt suit, and she pulled her hair back into a smooth French twist. She wore mascara and lipstick, and the boys and even the girls in her class adored her.

One day she was called to the office and told she must pack her things and leave immediately.

She'd lied to get the job.

"You have to tell white lies to survive," she said as she drove us home, back to our apartment. "I was doing it for us. Doing it for you kids."

"Will you go to hell?" I asked. The Catholic school had given me a newfound concern for all of our souls. I hoped she didn't die before making it to confession.

"Lying is a venial sin," my brother said with annoyance. "You don't go to hell for a venial sin."

"It's not a lie if you tell someone something," our mother said, "then, in your own mind, finish with this line: 'As far as you're concerned.'"

I was on her side because everybody talked about what a good teacher she was. Many of her students' grades had improved under her guidance, and one boy who couldn't read a word had quickly moved from first-grade to second-grade readers.

"You can't go back there." She stopped at an intersection, then gunned the car, transmitting her anger to the gas pedal. "We'll have to find you a new school."

That day marked the true beginning of our nomadic lifestyle. Within a year we'd lived in an apartment, a house, a trailer, another apartment. We went from public school, to Catholic school, back to public, all the while remaining in and around Burlington. Our mother got a job as a desk clerk at the Burlington Holiday Inn, and soon her coworkers and the salesmen who arrived from exotic locations became her new family.

It almost seemed our apartment had a revolving door, the men came and went so quickly. Some were nice, but many were loud and scary. Babysitters could no longer be afforded, and I was often left in charge of my younger brother, our mother coming home when the sun was rising. Days consisted of drama and rage and tears, of cheap engagement rings thrown as far as they could be thrown, of broken promises and men who lied, claiming to be single when they were really married.

As far as you're concerned.

Every man was the man of her life. It seemed that every one proposed, and every one was a wedding that never happened. Most of the men lasted weeks, but a few lasted months.

"We're getting out of here," my mother announced one day. These were words we were used to hearing with such regularity that most of our belongings never made it out of boxes that had become soft from our repeated moves.

"To Albuquerque, New Mexico."

Since the divorce we'd never ventured much beyond the boundaries of Burlington. Now she was talking about moving far away.

"Boyd lives in New Mexico, so it only makes sense that we should move there."

I'd heard this kind of talk before, enough to know it wouldn't happen, and Boyd, the newest boyfriend, would one day disappear to be replaced by someone else. But this time was different. This time my mother rented a U-Haul trailer and had a hitch welded to the bumper of our green Rambler. Once we realized a big move was truly in our future, we became excited. Even my baby brother, who was now three, felt the thrill of a new adventure. But I was sad to leave my grandma Florence, the only person who came to see us off, still wearing an apron, hands clasped tightly in front of her.

She and I had grown close, and our relationship was one more thing my mother found an intolerable reminder of the man who'd left her. I'd never seen Florence cry or show much emotion at all, but I detected tears in her eyes as the Rambler pulled away from the curb.

A trip by wagon train couldn't have been much harder. Instead of outposts, we traveled from one roadside motel to another, the journey interrupted by flat tires, a faulty hitch, an uneven load, an overheated engine, and a hysterical woman at the wheel of the car and at the wheel of our lives. And when the landscape turned alien and the sky became huge, my brothers and I watched from the backseat in silence and awe. No trees, no grass, just a vastness that was impossible to comprehend, that made me feel untethered, made me feel like I might fall or drift away.

On day five of the adventure, our mother made an announcement: "We're out of money."

It was another common line, but this time she really meant it. "Even if we don't have another breakdown, even if we go without eating, we won't have enough money for gas."

We were at a Stuckey's, parked in the shade of a Greyhound bus. The Rambler's windows were down, and our damp hair was plastered to our foreheads, our cheeks red from the heat.

She grabbed the steering wheel with both hands and began to sob. "I wish I were dead!" she wailed.

"Can you call Boyd?" my brother asked.

"No! He doesn't know we're coming. I wanted to surprise him!"

I waited a few moments, then ventured, "I have money."

The sobbing stopped. She turned and looked over the seat at me. "How much?"

"I don't know. Birthday money. From Grandma." My brother was smart; he always spent his gift money. I saved every dime. My mother had a notebook of all the money she'd borrowed, money she said she would pay back someday *with interest*. "I'll be just like the bank," she'd told me. "Only better."

But I'd finally started lying about how much I had. *As far as you're concerned*. I was pretty sure I would never get any of it back.

"Where?" she asked.

"Packed. In the trailer."

"Is it change? Is it just pennies?"

"Some pennies and some dimes and quarters and paper money." It would all be gone once I gave it to her. I knew that. But this was important. I was coming to the rescue.

We unloaded the trailer right there in the parking lot. Everything we owned.

"What box is it in?"

I couldn't remember. But I'd written my name on all of my boxes. "The fruit box. The one with oranges on it." No. Not it. "Maybe the toilet-paper box. It's in my little purse. The black one with the strings that pull." I was beginning to wish I'd never mentioned the money, because my mother was working herself into a frenzy. What if we never found it? I would be in so much trouble.

"Why did you pack it? Why would you pack money?"

I didn't want to admit I'd been hiding it from her, but I think she knew.

There were only a few boxes left in the trailer by the time we found it, all of us soaked with sweat. Twenty-three dollars. Money I'd squirreled away for years.

Now that our mother had it in her hands, there was no more talk about writing it down in the little notebook she kept for her debts. The notebook existed; she'd shown it to me once. A list of names and dates and the money borrowed. Even the baby was listed, but most of the entries consisted of my name, some small amounts, less than a dollar, but others were five and ten and even twenty.

Even though it was hot and we were physically miserable, our mother's mood improved now that our fortune had changed. "Look at this." She surveyed our belongings scattered around us in the parking lot. She laughed, and we all joined her. Even if I never saw the money again, the evaporation of her black mood was worth every cent. With joy and hope and renewed energy, we repacked the trailer. We would make it to Albuquerque.

Boyd was going to be so surprised and excited to see us. I tried to picture him, but his face blurred in my mind, and I confused him with the other boyfriends.

"Why are we going so slow?" my older brother asked. "Everybody's passing us."

The Rambler labored to pull the trailer up the steady incline, cars and semis roaring around us. "We're in the Rocky Mountains," our mother said. She pointed. "Look. That must be Sandia Peak. There's snow even though it's summer. Boyd told me about it. He wants to take all of us there. We'll go skiing and snowshoeing."

Her excitement was contagious, and we all sat forward, staring out the window at the strange surroundings, the wind bringing with it the smell of the desert mixed with the odor of exhaust fumes. When she was happy, we were happy. That's what our lives were about now, ever since the divorce. Trying to keep her happy, trying to stay out of her way, trying to be good.

I thought New Mexico was ugly, but I would never say so out loud. Maybe it was prettier in the mountains. Maybe more like home. Maybe the mountains had grass and trees.

We finally reached an area where the road leveled out and the little car no longer labored to pull its load. And then we were heading downhill. Below us a city spread from horizon to horizon.

The car picked up speed.

Our mother looked in the rearview mirror, alarm in her eyes. "I can't slow down." Behind us, the trailer swayed, the weight of it pushing the car forward as we descended into the valley. I smelled rubber burning and heard the sound of gears grinding. We began to slow, and the trailer quit swaying. We all breathed a sigh of relief.

At the edge of town, we pulled into a gas station, stopping a few feet from a phone booth. Even the gas station was ugly, with broken glass, and weeds growing from cracks. Our mother shut off the engine and opened her door. "Wait here while I make the call." She dug in her purse and pulled out some coins. "Fifty cents. That's all we have left. Can you believe it?" She laughed in delight. We were here. We'd made it with enough money to call Boyd.

All three of us bounced up and down.

She gave us one final, ravishing smile, left the car, and stepped into the phone booth, closing the door behind her as we watched through the glass.

We saw her drop the money in the slot and dial the number. She grasped the receiver, looked out the door, spotted us, and waved, her eyes sparkling.

It had taken us five days, but we were here. Tired and dirty and hungry, but we were here. I began to imagine the next few hours. We would eat, and we would be taken to a nice house. Would I have a bed of my own, or would I have to share with my younger brother? That would be okay for a while, but my mother had promised me a room of my own, with matching sheets and pillowcases. I wanted a canopy bed. Would I have a canopy bed? Pink, with ruffles. Cozy and safe. I would unpack my stuffed animals, and they would join me there.

We could see that someone had answered her call. She was talking, and her lips were moving. We saw the smile falter and the light in her eyes vanish. There was more talking, fast now, angry. Oh, how familiar we were with that sudden shift. She was shouting and crying. We could hear her raised voice but couldn't tell what she was saying. She slammed the receiver, then jerked open the phone-booth door. All three of us sank down in the backseat, trying to make ourselves as small as possible. The driver's door opened, and her rage and despair filled the car as she slid behind the wheel, sobbing deeply now.

We waited, but I don't think she even remembered we were there. Finally my older brother braved a question: "What happened?"

"He lied to me! He's not getting a divorce. His daughter answered the phone! Everything was a lie!"

"So we aren't going to his house?" I asked.

"No!" She swung around to glare at me, her teeth gritted in anger. "How can we live at his house? He's married! His wife and kids live there! He lied. He lied to all of us. Dirty, stinking, lying creep!"

No food. No bed.

My younger brother had been struggling to keep his tears to himself, but now he let loose, sobbing in terror. "I'm hungry!"

"Shhh," I said, pumping his little stick arm, trying to get him to stop crying. "We'll be okay. See if you can find a dime under the seat. If you find a dime, I'll buy you something at the gas station."

He stopped sobbing and began his hunt.

My mother blew her nose and wiped her face. She brushed her hair and pulled a tube of gold lipstick from her purse, turned the rearview mirror, quickly applied one, two, three swipes, capped the lipstick, and blotted with a tissue. "He's coming," she explained, dropping the lipstick tube back in her purse. "I told him we didn't have anyplace to stay and nothing to eat. He's going to put us up in a motel."

"Do you think he'll really come?" I asked.

"He'd better. Otherwise I'll call his house and tell his wife everything."

He came. It took forever, but he finally showed up. He was no longer the happy-go-lucky guy from Burlington. This man looked worried and sick, his shoulders hunched, the armpits of his shirt soaked with sweat. He didn't talk to me or my brothers, but I caught him looking at us with an expression of horror and guilt.

Boyd lived in an area of Albuquerque called the Heights. He found us a place to live in the Valley, as far from his house as we could possibly get. He stocked our refrigerator and cupboard with food, paid for a month's rent, then disappeared.

CHAPTER THIRTEEN

A honking horn woke me from a restless sleep.

It was a Cadillac horn, which is similar to a barge horn. You know these things when you've lived near the Mississippi River.

Outside the small house, the horn honked again and sleep fell away completely. I was in bed at Curtis Orchard, my new husband beside me.

Adrian started to get up, then fell back against the pillow. "The shower. I forgot about the shower."

The bedside radio said six o'clock. *In the morning.* I tried to figure out what a shower had to do with the car outside our house, but I couldn't put it together. Even if I'd been wide-awake, I'm not sure I could have solved the puzzle.

"I forgot to tell you my mother is having a shower this morning. It's something she and her friends do whenever one of their kids gets married."

"A shower? You mean like a wedding shower? She doesn't even know me."

"I'm sorry." He sat up and lit a cigarette, tossing out the match in the ashtray next to the bed. "I was supposed to tell you." He took a deep drag, then exhaled. "Doesn't matter if she doesn't know you. My mother is all about tradition and keeping up appearances."

I used to think my life was really messed up and that there was this whole world out there of normal people that I would never be a part of, that I would never understand. But I was beginning to wonder if I'd had it backwards.

I swung my legs over the side of the bed, slipped on my white cotton panties, and reached for my jeans. "I'm not going to any breakfast shower. You might want to tell her that."

"My God, you're beautiful."

I looked over my shoulder to see him staring at me all dreamy eyed and hungover. "You're just telling me that so I'll go." Or was he saying it so I'd forgive him for last night?

He lightly touched my back with calloused fingertips. "I would never do that."

I found my bra and put it on. That was followed by a green top with long flowing sleeves that I'd picked up at a head shop in Iowa City. "Well, I'm not beautiful, so you can quit trying to sweet-talk me."

I squeezed around to his side of the bed to peek out the window, pulling the muslin curtain aside a fraction of an inch. I groaned and dropped the fabric. "The car is full of people."

He grabbed my hand, and I turned to look at him. He was propped against the pillow, covered to the waist with the white sheet. I should have been in bed too. We should have slowly woken up together.

"Come on," he said. "Just go."

I reached for his cigarette. He handed it to me; I took two puffs, blowing smoke at the ceiling. "What kind of person doesn't even ask someone if she wants a shower?"

"A controlling person."

I passed the cigarette back. If I didn't go, his mother would hate me forever. She might hate me forever no matter what, but not going left no wiggle room.

"In three hours it will all be over," he said. "Three hours."

I'd already forgiven him. I was still smitten, and it would take more than one or two screwups to change my feelings.

Sandals and a finger-brush of my cropped hair, grab my shoulder bag, and I was out the door.

Giant white Caddy in the driveway.

The sun was barely up, but the light was harsh and brittle. Dew dampened the hem of my jeans, and a blue haze clung to grass and cornstalks in the nearby field.

I love that smell. The smell of corn. Not kernels of corn but the plant, the leaves. That humid, organic scent that wraps around your head and comforts you. It's heavy and it's rich, like nothing else I've ever smelled in my life. If perfume smelled like that, I would wear it.

The car was packed. Four people in the front seat, three in the back.

Too late to change my mind; they were all looking at me. It felt like I was in some play, already onstage. My job was to fake it, just get through until the final curtain. Head low, mouth shut.

I wasn't a fashion queen, and I didn't think of myself as a fashion snob, but I'd never seen so much pastel and polyester packed into one vehicle in my life. White slacks with sharp creases. Floral perfume and hair that had just come out of hot rollers.

I squeezed in back with three girls who were probably a few years older than I was. The girl beside me recoiled. I'd forgotten to brush my teeth. *Sorry.* Did I have tobacco on my mouth? I picked at my bottom lip, but my fingers came away clean.

I could tell they were shocked by my unkempt appearance. The girls gave me an uncomfortable *hi*, and one even shot me a look of sympathy.

My new mother-in-law made introductions as she drove, very badly.

They talked about wedding things, and babies and baby showers. Ruth explained to them that I hadn't registered my pattern yet, but I would soon.

My *pattern?*

I wanted to say that my pattern was Kmart melamine with a little pawnshop thrown in, but I was pretty sure nobody would think it funny. This was serious married stuff, serious homemaker stuff. You didn't joke about that.

It was thirty minutes to Burlington, so that gave them time to do what none of them would ever call shoot the shit.

Mothers and daughters gave me sly, sidelong, hopeful glances.

Oh, they were enjoying this. Not because they were enjoying torturing me. I meant nothing to them. No, they were enjoying the pain my very existence brought to my new mom.

Interesting.

The glances grew bolder, dropping to my stomach.

A baby. Now, *that* was funny.

A few tentative questions came my way—shy attempts to start conversations. All topics I knew nothing about that had to do with taking care of the home, and cooking, and thread counts and monogrammed towels. How to hang curtains, and Electrolux vacuum cleaners. Tupperware and who was at church last Sunday and who would be teaching Bible school this year. There was talk of baby showers and 4-H and something called Homemakers' Extension.

Much of the conversation from the front seat was gossip disguised as concern, and once it was obvious I would be no help in any of it, my presence was ignored and I could just sit back and listen. I dropped into observer mode while trying to sort out the mood in the car.

We approached my uncle's bar, and conversation dwindled and died.

If there had been any train tracks in the vicinity, the bar would have been on the wrong side of them.

As we passed, all heads turned. I could feel my mother-in-law's shame and the combined horror and pleasure of her friends. The sign read BLUE RIBBON SPECIAL.

The car moved on, away from that uncomfortable situation within an uncomfortable situation. We floated under black oaks, the branches creating a strobe effect. A turn to the west and we were off the bluff, dipping into the bottoms, where the soil was black and fertile and where the river had once been miles wide. Cultivated crops flashed past windows until we reached a metal span that connected Illinois to Iowa.

"I hate this bridge." The breathless words came from the girl beside me.

Arm to arm, I felt the tension in her body as the steel trembled beneath us.

I loved the bridge.

It was like a rickety midway ride put together by strung-out carnies. Every time you got on, you just didn't know. This could be it. Your number could be up. Would it collapse this time?

Odds were it wouldn't, but there was always that tiny chance, and that tiny chance always gave me a rush.

Once we reached solid ground, the girl beside me relaxed.

Burlington, Iowa. Home of Aldo Leopold, Snake Alley, and poor city planners.

It used to be magnificent, with beautiful Victorian homes clinging to majestic bluffs overlooking the Mississippi River. But most of that was gone. People had decided to rip out the heart of the small city, bulldozing hundreds of historic homes to put in a new road that led to sprawl, strip malls, and the rest of Iowa. The people who stayed got to witness a death rattle that would last a century, and the people who came would never know what they'd missed. But if they were sensitive, they might feel the whisper of it in a brick alley or on a forgotten corner.

The total disregard for the beauty of the past hurt me deep in my bones. Why don't people stop? Just stop? Does it take so much to *just stop*? I wasn't talking about solving world problems or coming up with a better idea. Just stop the destruction.

But who was I to judge or complain?

The breakfast took place in the downtown Hotel Burlington. The hostess ushered us to a small banquet room with a white tablecloth and white napkins folded in wedges and placed on fine china.

We ordered. We ate.

It was even more awkward than I'd anticipated.

People gave me gifts. Complete strangers gave me gifts.

Things that left me baffled as to function and use. A silver tray. A crystal vase. A lot of crystal. Crystal impressed the new mom. Shiny stuff. Someone gave me a set of pretty etched plates with glass teacups that fit into outlines on the plates.

Seeing my perplexity, one of the girls explained, "They're for homemaker parties and receptions. They hold your dessert and coffee."

I didn't have homemaker parties and receptions. That wasn't me. That would never be me.

But it seemed a mandatory part of this new life, and I could already feel the tedium of it sucking the soul right out of me—just this brief glimpse of their strangely fascinating world of misguided importance. Here a woman's role was to take care of the house and have babies. And the women didn't resent it. They embraced it.

On the return trip, as I thought of all the strange booty I'd scored at the shower, we passed my uncle's bar again. This time Uncle Jim was outside puttering around, waist deep in weeds and junk cars.

And I suddenly caught a faint whiff of my mother-in-law's horror. Just for a fraction of a second, I almost understood her.

My uncle—someone I'd always seen as an eccentric genius— changed as I imagined him through her eyes.

White trash. He was white trash.

I suddenly saw the situation from Ruth's perspective. Her son had married an outsider, someone beneath him.

White trash.

Stunned, I swallowed and looked away, and a seed of doubt was planted.

That's how easily it happens.

Less than twenty-four hours into this new life, my self-perception was shifting. Already I was asking myself if my world had really been what I'd thought. Maybe all of the crystal and silver trays and talk about curtains was the way real people lived. The way they were supposed to live.

That's how easy it was to start wondering if they were right and I was wrong.

A crop duster buzzed a nearby cornfield.

When the pilot reached the highway, he shut off the cloud of spray and throttled up, the plane roaring skyward to circle for another approach. It was a beautiful ballet, the yellow plane against the blue sky, the music of the engine, the green of the corn. The spray hung suspended in the air above the fields, then drifted toward us.

The heavy odor of pesticide crept in through the car vents. It touched white slacks and hair that had been set on rollers. It fell against soft cheeks and dark, shy lashes.

The mothers and daughters carried on as if nothing unusual were taking place anywhere outside or inside the car. They were caught up in talk of babies. Talk of family. Talk of the future.

CHAPTER FOURTEEN

The next afternoon, I answered a knock to find a stocky female dressed in jeans and a gray T-shirt standing on the front step. She looked about twenty-five, with a sunburned face and shoulder-length brown hair.

"You must be Adrian's new wife." Like somebody hitchhiking, she pointed over her shoulder with her thumb. "I'm your neighbor, Connie. I run my parents' farm now that they've retired."

"By yourself?" She became instantly more interesting.

"By myself."

There seemed to be two main types of farm women. The homemakers who had little to do with farming, and the women who worked right alongside the men. Connie looked like she could toss a bale of hay as high as any guy could.

"I know you had one of those boring breakfast showers," she said. "I would have come, but I wasn't invited. Here—got you a little something." She handed me a package wrapped in pink tissue paper, tied at both ends with white curling ribbon.

I tried to imagine Connie packed into the car with us but couldn't. "I'm sorry you weren't invited to the shower, but it was pretty awful."

Following me inside, she laughed, and the sound was deep and robust. "I'll bet." She nodded toward the gift. "Go on. Open it."

The paper tore easily. "Oh, a rolling pin." Heavy and wooden.

"Do you already have one?"

"No." It had been years since I'd used a rolling pin. "Thank you," I said, touched by the gift.

"If you live on an apple farm, you have to have a rolling pin."

It was understandable that the locals were curious about me, and she was staring in a way that made me uncomfortable. I wasn't sure if I wanted her to sit down, so I lingered near the front door.

"I heard Adrian married a girl he hardly knew," she said, getting directly to the point without wasting time on idle chitchat. "The whole county is buzzing about it. But Adrian isn't a spur-of-the-moment kind of guy. He thinks things through, then thinks them through again."

"So you're trying to figure out why he married me?" What a horribly rude person. She should have thought twice about giving me a rolling pin.

She tipped her head and examined me. "You're kind of interesting. Cute in an innocent way. That might have appealed to Adrian. Have you ever lived on a farm?"

"No, but I've lived near them."

She shook her head and smiled. Almost laughed. "This is just so odd. I mean, I've known Adrian all my life. Our parents were best friends until they had a falling-out several years ago. I'm telling you, this is totally out of character." She paused, examining my face again. "And yet... He sometimes gets a wild hare and will do something off the wall to get a reaction out of people."

Why was she doing this? Was she just a mean, nasty person who was mad because she hadn't been invited to the shower, or was she trying to warn me about farm life? Probably a little of both.

"You won't last. If you haven't grown up on a farm, you won't make it here. One day you'll pack your bags and be thankful to put this place behind you."

I wadded up the wrapping paper until it was a tight ball. "Did you ever date Adrian?" I asked with suspicion. She might be a bitter old girlfriend.

"Growing up, we were more like brother and sister. Although I have to confess to having a crush on him back when we were in middle school. Who wouldn't? The guy is gorgeous."

I wasn't buying that she didn't still like him.

"But honestly?" Connie said. "You aren't his type. You really aren't."

I managed to make it to the couch, setting the rolling pin and wrapping paper aside, company briefly unimportant.

I'd known. Of course I'd known. Good things didn't happen to me, but couldn't a girl pretend that a guy loved her? Couldn't a girl fool herself for longer than a few days?

Connie followed and sat one cushion away, her cheeks flushing bright red under the sunburn. She looked distressed, which was ridiculous because my reaction couldn't have been unexpected. Did she think I'd embrace her revelations?

"I'm so sorry," she said. "Please forget everything I said."

Forget? "Hey, I appreciate the information." Trying for casual, I reached for a pack of cigarettes and lit up, surprised that my hands weren't shaking. "I'd like to know more. I'd like to know everything." I inhaled deeply and blew out a cloud of smoke. It wasn't enough to take the edge off, but it was something to fiddle with while I pulled myself together. Gradually I became aware of Connie's voice. I think she'd been talking a long time.

"He was dating a girl…Supposed to get married. I'm not sure what happened." Connie seemed to consider her next words, then shifted her weight and leaned closer in a confiding pose. "Adrian was crazy about her."

"Was her name Melinda?"

"I think so."

I don't know why I struggled to maintain an outward appearance of calm. Habit, I guess. Protection. Don't let them know they're hurting you. I could feel my heart settling down, and I could feel my emotions taking a backseat.

"Now that I think of it, his old girlfriend looked quite a bit like you, and she worked at a bar. Didn't you and Adrian meet at a bar?"

"Yes." I didn't want to believe her, I wasn't ready to believe her, but she'd set in motion a lot of doubt.

"Everybody is talking about the marriage."

"You already said that."

"Well, I'm saying it again because that could be a motive behind this stunt."

Now it was a stunt.

"Nothing Adrian's mom would hate more than everybody in the county gossiping and speculating about her son's marriage and new wife."

I thought about yesterday, when we'd driven past my uncle's bar. How humiliated Ruth had been. And how the other women had relished it.

Connie was gloating a little herself. Trying to contain her excitement over the odd event that was the talk of the community.

"Maybe he cares about me," I heard myself say. "Maybe we'll move away from here and find our own place."

She shook her head and chuckled. "That will never happen. Never. That's what I mean. If you haven't grown up on a farm, you don't understand how it works. He won't leave. He *can't* leave. He's the eldest son. He was born here, and he'll die here."

I couldn't decide if I liked Connie or hated her. I knew I should hate her, but there was something oddly refreshing about her directness, even if I was unsure of the motive behind it. Maybe she'd been stuck away in the boonies too long. Maybe she was just socially inept. And at least I was getting some version of Adrian's life and of farm culture, even at the risk of it being skewed.

"You certainly aren't what I expected—I know that," she said.

"What did you expect?"

"Someone with a lot of curves. Big boobs. Blond hair and a ton of makeup. That's what I expected. The kind of girl who blinds a man for a while. Until he gets his fill of her and wonders what the hell he was thinking. But you..."

She didn't say it. She didn't have to. I was a mouse. A little gray mouse. And why would Adrian marry a mouse when he could have the pick of almost any woman in the area?

"Maybe Adrian *is* crazy about you." She gave my arm a quick, reassuring squeeze. "Maybe that's all there is to it. Maybe it was love at first sight."

"Yeah. Maybe." But Connie had tapped into my own repressed concerns, and my response was hollow.

"Adrian can be a self-centered workaholic," she said. "If you need a night out, give me a call or just stop by. We could even do something domestic like bake an apple pie. We'll bake a pie, and you can bring it home to Adrian as a surprise. He used to love Granny Smiths or any of those early tart apples. He loves cherry pie too."

She knew more about my husband than I did. She could have answered my grandmother's questions.

Connie got up and headed for the door, eager to be off. God knew she'd done enough damage.

"You'll come?" she asked.

Before Connie's visit, I'd been able to fool myself into thinking everything would be fine. But she'd filled in blanks that I hadn't wanted filled. She'd brought a blunt truth, and along with that truth a darkness that might never lift. And in that moment I understood that I'd stepped into a world I could never be a part of.

I looked at Connie. At her strong tan arms and dusty boots. I thought about Adrian and his mother and the farm. This wasn't me. None of this was me.

She was in the doorway now.

"One mile if you go through the fields. Walk out your front door and turn left; cross the hard road to the lane that runs along the creek. Follow that until you hit a rusty DeKalb sign. Turn south and go a quarter mile. You'll come right up in my backyard. If the dog is out, don't pay any attention to her. She'll bark, but she won't bite."

How could I have imagined being able to step into this strange life? Subconsciously, I'd thought of it as a temporary role. Farm wife. I'd never thought about the consequences. I'd never thought about a year from now, or even a month from now. Everything for me was transient. And I'd been infatuated. I was still infatuated.

But this was real.

These people were real.

This life was real.

Not my life. It would never be my life.

CHAPTER FIFTEEN

I would stay. For a while. At least that's what I told myself. It felt like lingering, biding my time, waiting to see if things changed or improved or got bad enough to justify a packed suitcase. I spent days alone. Evenings alone. I would wait and wait, and he would never come home. Not until I'd gone to bed and turned out the lights. And there he would be, fumbling for me in the dark. He would rise before dawn, gone before I woke up.

Where did he go? What did he do when he wasn't at our house?

It felt as though I'd been stuck away in a box, and he just came around when he wanted sex.

I'd never had any desire to be a wife.

Ugh.

A horrid word. *Wife.* It implied ownership. And now I was acting like a whiny wife. I'd seen it on television and in movies. Where the wife was always nagging the husband. *Husband.* Another unappealing word. But in those stories, the guy was usually up to something. Like having an affair. How had my life become such a cliché, and in such a short time?

If there was another woman, it would mean he'd met her and they'd hooked up right after he and I were married. How was that possible?

Unless it was someone he'd known before...

Yes.

The girl he'd almost married. Or someone else. Another old flame. He had them. His mother had told me. With relish.

"Where have you been?" I'd asked him several times in our short marriage when he would show up with a bundle of clothes tucked under his arm. He'd never moved in. All of his belongings were still at his parents' house. "How can you farm in the dark? How can you feed cattle in the dark?"

He'd dismissed me with words and a look of disdain. "You don't know anything about farming."

That was true, but something wasn't right. A lot wasn't right, but this was more. This was big. I could feel it deep in my belly—a darkness and a sense that if I peeled away what was on top, I would find something I didn't want to find.

I heard his truck.

Already my ears could distinguish it from the other vehicles that rolled past. The engine was steady, the exhaust loud.

It didn't stop. Didn't pull into the driveway.

Sitting on the bed in the dim light, I kept my ears tuned. The sound of the truck faded, then grew a little louder. It slowed, then shut off.

Not at our house.

Did it really matter? What he did? Where he went? I tried not to let it bug me, but that wasn't going to happen. I waited, expecting to hear the crunch of boots on gravel, expecting to hear the kitchen door open and close.

Nothing.

Dinner was on the table. It had been on the table for an hour. Just like every other night.

I stabbed out my cigarette, finished my beer. I would see if I could find him. I would venture from the house into his world.

Outside, the sky was black and the air was cool against my bare arms. I heard cattle bawling in the distance. Not a nervous kind of bawling, but just kind of milling around. Maybe a cow calling her calf.

Across the road at the big two-story farmhouse, lights burned in windows. I stuck my hands in the pockets of my jeans and moved closer. When I hit the grass, my footsteps silenced. I cut through bushes and ducked under the clothesline where the cider-press cloths hung. They smelled sweet and sour—like apples and vinegar.

There was a little patio outside the kitchen. I clung to the deeper shadows of trees and bushes. From there, I could see through the window. There they were, like a Norman Rockwell painting, sitting at the kitchen table. Mother. Father.

Son.

Sitting at the table eating supper. Talking and smiling.

How incredibly odd.

I couldn't process what I was seeing. I just stood and watched, thinking the image had to change, or that I had to be having some kind of hallucination.

But no. There was my new husband, sitting and eating with his family.

This was where he went every night. This was why I never saw him. Yes, there was another woman. His mother.

If I returned to our little house, he would eventually show up and poke around at dinner, never admitting that he'd already eaten. I almost laughed when I thought about the weight he'd put on in the short time we'd been married.

Playing house. That's what he was doing. What we were doing. Because I couldn't blame him for everything. After all, I'd married a guy I didn't even know. My uncle had warned me. My grandmother had warned me. And now I was witnessing his real life through the kitchen window.

The only times I'd been inside the house had been when Adrian was with me. On the few occasions when I'd attempted visits without him, I hadn't been invited in.

I still thought of myself as a kid, and I'd had a lot of practice shutting out people like them. But this... This involved Adrian.

Why had he married me? I didn't get it, and I needed to get it. Needed to understand.

I stood staring at them for a long time, feeling as though I were watching through a lens.

Had it been hormones and sex? I hated to think there had been no other connection, that our mating was no more than an unconscious effort to procreate. But it seemed that was the case. And yet I couldn't help but feel cheated. He'd represented the most normal of existences to me. The kind of normal I'd craved my entire life.

I'd had bad dreams like this, where even as the dreamer I was aware of the lack of logic. But this was real. This was really happening. It was part of the darkness I'd been sensing. But not all of the darkness. I was pretty sure I'd uncovered just a little, and I was pretty sure I didn't want to uncover any more.

I had no desire to confront them. I just wanted out; I'd had enough of their crazy bullshit. I don't know why I hadn't left before. Maybe because I actually cared for him. Or maybe because I was young, foolish, and romantic, even though I hated to admit to believing in love and romance. That was a weakness.

One thing I knew—a guy had no business getting married when he was still on the teat.

CHAPTER SIXTEEN

I ran back to the small house. Inside, I pulled out my suitcase and tossed in my clothes.

I slammed the suitcase shut and latched the latches, grabbed the handle, my purse, my keys, my cigarettes, and ran out the back door. I would worry about my other things later.

I shoved the suitcase behind the front seat, jumped into the car, and turned the ignition key. I had two exit choices: sneak away quietly with no lights, or fly out of there like the devil was after me. I wanted to choose number two, but with my heart slamming in my chest, I restrained myself. Instead of tromping down on the accelerator, I coasted past the big farmhouse, wincing at the sound of tires rolling over gravel. As I turned left on the blacktop surface, I locked the driver's door, then reached across and locked the passenger side.

I don't know what I thought was going to happen, why I thought I needed to protect myself. But I was afraid. Irrationality of such magnitude scared the hell out of me.

I wasn't sure where I was going. *Away* was the only thought I had. Away from Adrian. Away from the farm.

When I reached Highway 34, I hit the headlights and made another left. In less than a minute, I was in third gear doing sixty.

Until that moment I hadn't realized I was shaking.

Where was I going? My uncle's? No, I couldn't face him. Not right now. Not when he'd tried to talk me out of getting married in the first place. I could go to my grandmother's, but I'd shown up on her doorstep too many times.

I just wanted to drive and keep driving.

My entire world was the interior of the car. I didn't want to think of anything beyond the doors. Everything he'd said, every gesture, every touch, every smile, had meant nothing.

And yet something close to a sense of relief came over me. Like answering a curious question that had been lurking in the back of my mind. It wasn't me; it was *him*.

I suddenly realized I was driving. I'd forgotten I was behind the wheel until I caught a dark movement in my right peripheral vision. At that same moment I felt a violent impact, followed by the sound of metal scraping across the surface of the road.

The windshield shattered.

The hood crumpled.

The car spun in slow motion, the rear sliding, sparks flying until it came to a jarring halt. I sat there, hands gripping the wheel. Gradually I became aware of the smell of antifreeze, gasoline, and motor oil. The hiss of hot water. Gradually I became aware of my ragged breathing and the darkness that surrounded me.

I fumbled for the handle. Pulled. Nothing. I slammed my shoulder against the door. Nothing.

I rolled down the window and dove out, falling to the ground, gravel cutting my palms and knees. Beyond the roar in my head, beyond my own thundering heart, came another sound.

A horrible sound.

An animal in agony.

I could see a darker shape on the road.

Deer?

No, it didn't sound like a deer.

Cow?

It was suffering. That was all I knew.

Someone please come and help.

My arms and legs shook uncontrollably, but I managed to shove myself to my feet. Two cars drove past, slowed, then sped up. Several minutes later I heard a siren in the distance. The gawkers must have called the police. Flashing lights appeared around the bend, pulling to a stop in front of a tangled mass of guts. I turned away, still unsure of what I'd hit.

The officer checked on me first. "Are you hurt?"

"No. I don't know. I don't think so."

Everything had happened so quickly that I suppose I could have been hurt, but I didn't feel anything. Nothing but the violent, almost comical shaking. It didn't seem real. If someone were to exaggerate being cold, this would be it.

I realized my mouth and fingers were numb, and when I talked, my tongue felt weird. Frozen and thick. "You h-have to h-help th-that animal." I pointed but didn't look.

"Anyone else with you?"

"No."

Two more police cars showed up. One officer pulled out a handgun, approached the thrashing animal, and fired three times. The cries of agony stopped.

He put away his weapon and walked back to where the other officer and I stood along the road. "What a mess." He sounded sick.

"A cow?" I asked hopefully. I don't know why it seemed less horrid to have killed a cow, but it did. I guess because cows were slaughter animals.

"Horse."

A horse...

He pulled out a notepad and began taking down information for his report. Without even thinking, I gave him my maiden name. If I had thought, I probably would have done the same, because to me, Mrs. Adrian Curtis was someone else. Mrs. Adrian Curtis wasn't me.

"We should call an ambulance."

"No, I'm okay."

I'd had a lot of practice pretending I was okay, pretending I wasn't messed up when I really was, so I was able to convince the cop that I hadn't been seriously injured. I would assess myself later.

"Then a relative or friend."

I gave him my uncle's name and number.

Tears suddenly burned my eyes, and I blinked rapidly to clear my vision. I wiped the back of my hand against my nose. I was crying about the animal I'd killed, and I was crying about my uncle and our damaged relationship. I was crying about Adrian.

Another cop car showed up, lights flashing. Officers began setting up emergency lights and directing traffic. Someone wrapped a blanket around me and led me to a police car and helped me into the passenger side.

"Wait here."

I lost track of time, uncertain if minutes or hours had passed. I touched my scalp, and my fingers came away sticky.

My uncle was coming. He would be here soon. He would take care of me.

I thought about going back to the bar. I thought about opening my sofa bed and crawling between familiar sheets. I thought about the comforting clack of pool balls and the taste of beer from a bleached glass.

Home.

But it wouldn't be the same.

I wished I'd never come to this place. I wished I'd never joined my uncle in his lonely outpost. After what had happened, how could anything ever be right again? But things hadn't been right for a long time. Things hadn't been right since long before I'd eaten the mushroom.

It seemed as if I'd been in the police car forever when the door opened and the policeman stuck his head inside. "I called your uncle, but he said we should contact your husband instead."

I looked through the windshield. A truck was pulling sharply to the edge of the highway, gravel spewing, headlights momentarily blinding me. A man got out, and I recognized a familiar stride coming toward me.

Adrian.

CHAPTER SEVENTEEN

I sat in the cab of Adrian's truck, shivering even though the night was muggy and warm. In the headlights of the police car, the cop passed my battered suitcase to Adrian. I couldn't see his face, but I imagined his surprise, maybe even embarrassment and humiliation. Or did he play along? Yes, that's what he would do. Act as if the suitcase was no surprise. *My wife was on her way to visit a relative. My wife was on her way to the train station.* I *could* have been on my way to visit someone. I *could* have been on my way to somewhere.

Confusion clouded my brain, and I struggled to recall what had precipitated my drive.

The kitchen window. The kitchen table.

Yes. That was it. As soon as the memory entered my head, it floated away and became irrelevant. The poor horse, the wrecked car, other times when death had come knocking—those were the things right in front of me. Those were the things I focused on.

And the man walking toward me with the suitcase.

For a moment I couldn't place him. For a moment, I saw him with the eyes of a stranger. That first flush of interest. That hint of curiosity. *Who is that?*

Then I realized it was Adrian. *My husband.* But once I figured out who he was, he was still as unfamiliar as he'd been moments earlier when I'd thought he was a stranger.

Adrian hefted the suitcase into the bed of the truck. I felt it hit bottom—the vehicle shuddered—and I marveled that a single suitcase could be so heavy.

The driver's door creaked open, and Adrian slid behind the wheel.

"Your car is totaled." His voice was devoid of emotion, and I had no idea what he was thinking.

Just a car, but it had special meaning to me because it had been a gift from my uncle, something he'd won in a bet. A Mustang. A horse hitting a horse.

"What will happen to it?" I asked.

"A junkyard will tow it away."

Adrian turned the truck around, and we headed back in the direction of the farm. I felt a brief flutter of panic at the thought of returning to a place I'd left for good. And even though I'd run off in despair, I'd also experienced a feeling of relief at having put the orchard and Adrian behind me. We weren't even there yet, but already I could feel my world shrinking. And this time it would be smaller because I would have no car.

He lit a cigarette and tossed the pack on the dashboard. "You were leaving without even telling me. Why?"

I inhaled the toxic scent of burning tobacco. From his point of view, I'm sure my flight had no apparent trigger. I should have confronted him. I should have told him I was going, but I can be a coward at times. Now I felt foolish and immature. I'd run away like some idiot, and look what had happened. Even now, I could only blurt out the most direct and limited words necessary to get the message across. "I don't know why you married me."

He made a strange sound of shock and surprise. "Maybe I care about you."

"You still live at home. You still eat supper with your parents. *I saw you.*"

Anybody else would have been embarrassed at being caught. He acted as if the whole arrangement were perfectly normal. "That's what people do on a farm. They eat together and talk about the day. And honestly, I don't like the food you cook."

After getting married, it had surprised me to find that he'd grown up eating packaged and processed meals that could quickly go from the freezer to the oven or fryer, heavily seasoned with salt, pepper, and ketchup. I'd had no exposure to most of the food he liked. Having lived in New Mexico, I was more familiar with tamales and enchiladas, chiles rellenos and refried beans.

My childhood might have been unconventional, but most of the food I'd eaten had been prepared from scratch and had involved creativity. I'd brought that tradition to our meals, with disastrous results. I'd attempted to find out what kind of bland, boring food he liked and had somehow missed the mark there too. His tastes were very specific, and I learned that processed food fell into categories and subcategories of nastiness.

"You're just picky," I said. "Not liking my cooking is no reason to eat at your mother's. I really want to know why you married me, because what we have is not a marriage. Am I a breeder? Is that it?"

He let out a snort. "Why can't you believe I care about you?"

He didn't mention love. "Then let's leave." In my earnestness, I shifted to face him. "Let's go somewhere and start our own life. Together."

"That's impossible. That will never happen. The farm is my home. It's been in the family for over a hundred years. I'm not going anywhere. I'm not walking away from my history and my heritage."

"It's not my heritage." I hadn't understood how my lack of roots would alienate me on a daily basis. "Turn around. Take me to my uncle's." I had the overwhelming feeling that if I didn't leave now, I would never leave.

Our speed didn't change.

I reached for the door handle. "Stop the truck. Stop the truck or I'll jump out."

He laughed as if he found me incredibly amusing. "I'm sorry. It's just that you sound so melodramatic. Come on. Let's go home. Forget about tonight. I'll draw pictures of you when we get back."

Draw me? He was treating me like a child, and I probably did seem like a child to him. "I don't want you to draw any pictures of me. That would mean nothing now."

"But I married you. Doesn't that count for anything?"

He was confusing me. Making light of something I'd taken seriously. Was I overreacting to his eating dinner with his parents? "I was your protest. That's what I think."

He'd broken my heart—that's what he'd done. That's why I'd run away. I hadn't been able to face the thought of his not caring for me. Of just being some stray dog he'd brought home and then quickly forgotten. I wondered if that's what had happened. Had he forgotten I was there on the farm? Had he gone home and eaten with his parents, forgetting I even existed?

"So what if you're my protest? Not saying you are, but so what?"

"So what? That's mean! You're mean." I couldn't think straight. I'd just wrecked my car. I'd just killed a horse. I didn't want to have this conversation. He should have hugged me and told me how worried he'd been. How glad he was that I was alive. He'd done none of those things. Instead, he offered to draw me.

"Maybe I don't fully understand why I married you. There. Is that what you wanted to hear?"

"Of course not, but it's better than a lie." Truth was, he probably didn't know why he'd married me. "When you get married, that person should be number one in your life." Were we nothing more than two mixed-up people who'd unwisely chosen to pool our confusion? Two oddly drawn outsiders negatively impacted by our equally unusual upbringings?

"The farm is number one. The farm will always come first. I'm sorry. That's just the way it is."

A farm. I hadn't understood the rules that came with this new life. I'd been looking for tradition and family and security. And yes, love. Was that so shameful?

"We're different," he said. "You like to lay it all out there. I'm not like that."

"What about Melinda?"

"Who?"

"Melinda. The girl you almost married."

We were home now, pulling into the gravel-and-grass driveway. Adrian shut off the engine before the truck stopped rolling. "Her name was Matilda, and we were never engaged. She was a psycho, and when I dumped her she stalked me for months and told everybody I'd broken off our engagement."

Those certainly weren't the words I'd expected to hear.

CHAPTER EIGHTEEN

.

I took a hot shower, and when I was done, I slipped on a pair of flannel pajama bottoms and an old T-shirt. In the medicine cabinet mirror above the bathroom sink, I could see a bruise on my forehead, and I thought about my earlier confusion and how I hadn't recognized Adrian. I remembered when a neighbor had fallen and hit her head on the sidewalk, she'd acted very strange for a few days, with dizzy spells and memory problems.

In the living room, candles burned, and a small lamp glowed in the corner. The windows were open. From outside came the sound of crickets and the scent of damp earth and heavy dew. Ivory curtains billowed softly, made of fabric that changed according to movement and light. Just watching them made me aware of how they would feel sliding across my palm.

"Here." Adrian handed me a small package. "Sorry about the way it's wrapped."

I peeled the newspaper aside. A vintage nightgown. Long, off-white, thin straps, made of silk.

"I got it as a wedding present, but then I didn't know if you'd like it, so I didn't give it to you. I know you don't wear things like that—" He looked uncomfortable, as if the inappropriateness underscored how little he knew about me. But I loved vintage even though I rarely wore it.

He reached out to grab it back. I pulled it away, and his fingertips snagged on the delicate fabric.

"No, I love it. And you wanted to draw me."

I put on the gown in the bedroom because I didn't want him to see the transition from cotton to silk. I stripped off the practical clothes, then let the fabric slide over me, the hem falling to my knees. I wondered who had worn it last. Someone who was now very old, or someone who was dead.

Adrian was right—it was unlike anything I would ever wear. I could smell the fabric, like something that had been tucked away in a drawer for a long time, with hints of lavender and dust.

My brain felt cloudy, and confusion washed over me again.

Did it matter? Did any of it matter? Why did I care where he ate dinner? I struggled to figure out why any of it made any difference, and I couldn't even find my previous reaction to revisit.

Everything was cast in shadow. The closet door was ajar, and the clothes were undefined shapes with no color. The floor under my bare feet was uneven, hand hewn from pine trees, the mismatched edges rough beneath the round braid rug. The faded flower-print wallpaper could hardly be seen in the dim light, but I could smell the paper and old glue. One day I would scrape it off, and I would paint the wall with something fresh.

Or not.

Maybe I wouldn't change anything. Maybe I wouldn't put my touch on the place at all. Maybe I was the one who needed to adapt and adjust. Maybe the secret was to embrace the past. Accept and acknowledge the past, the history, the heritage, without bringing any of myself into the picture.

Maybe I didn't want or need to know what was under the wallpaper.

I touched the gown, as small and thin as a slip. I loved the way the fabric felt against my body. So foreign and unfamiliar. Yes, so unlike me. Like putting on someone else's skin.

The thoughts weren't typical of me—I was lucid enough to realize that. Almost like with a drug, different synapses were firing in my brain. It felt good to let go.

In the living room, Adrian was waiting. He sat in a wooden chair, floor lamp behind him to illuminate the sketch pad braced against his leg. A moth circled inside the white lampshade.

When Adrian saw me in the gown, I think he wanted to reach for me, pull me to him, but I walked by to curl up in the armchair on the opposite side of the small room. Two candles burned on the table, near enough for me to feel their heat and smell the melting wax.

My head hurt, but not badly. I was more aware of the air on my arms, and the cold fabric that caressed my body. Silk was so impractical. And why wouldn't it be? Something made by worms? I doubted that worms were the most practical creatures in the world.

I touched the cloth. "This is silk." Yes, I think the bump on my head was making me stupid.

He started drawing. "There are almost seventy species of silk moths."

I had the strange notion that when Adrian held a pencil in his hand he connected with who he was. He fell through a hole in the paper and entered another consciousness. And me? I was all about old wallpaper.

Maybe I was looking for romance, but I wasn't a romantic person. That might be because I'd witnessed the men who'd come and gone in my mother's life, and, even as a little kid, I'd known love wasn't a good thing. I'd seen the parade and knew that none of them cared about her. I think the man she married after my father was the only one who'd truly loved her, but I'm not even sure what he'd felt was love, because it was more of a desperate obsession. More of a clinging to something he knew he could never hang on to, no matter how strong his grip.

But somehow Adrian seemed casually able to stage romantic moments that didn't make me laugh.

He made me feel like someone else.

What a mystery to see his head bent over the sketchbook, see the shimmer of light on his hair and his face cast in shadow while the pencil lead softly scraped across the rough surface of the paper, and me with no idea of the image materializing on the blank sheet.

Would the drawing give any insight into his true feelings?

"Do you know I used to be left-handed?" he asked.

"How does a person go from being left-handed to right? Did you have an injury?"

He offered me a cigarette. I shook my head. He lit up and tossed the pack aside, blowing a cloud of smoke toward the ceiling before going back to the paper resting on his leg.

"My mother tied my left hand to my side every day until my right hand became dominant."

A wave of dizziness washed over me, dizziness that had nothing to do with my knock on the head.

"I was already drawing by that time. Just typical houses and those people with nothing but heads and legs that kids like to draw."

"You can remember that far back?"

"You tend to remember things like that, even if you're three. So anyway, I had to learn to use my right hand. It took a while, but I did it."

"I've heard a left-handed person's brain is wired differently. And that you should never force a person to change. Did she do it because she didn't want you to be different?"

"My mother has some strange notions. She's not the only one around here who thinks being born left-handed is the sign of evil. She thought she was protecting me."

"If you had a left-handed kid, would you tie his arm down?"

He looked up from the sketch pad. Hair fell across his forehead, and his eyes were shadowed. "No."

Again my thoughts turned to the old girlfriend. Even though I now knew the truth, I couldn't quit thinking about her. "Was I your do-over?"

He took a drag from the cigarette. "Can we not talk about people who are no longer in my life? This is about you and me."

He pinched the cigarette into his mouth and squinted against the smoke. "I'm done." He unfolded himself from the chair and handed the tablet to me.

A simple yet elegant line drawing. My legs tucked under me, a wistful hand beneath my chin, elbow on the table as I looked, not at Adrian but out the window into the night. The woman's face was thinner, the lips fuller, the hair wispier. But these were attributes a man might exaggerate, and the drawing was me.

"It's lovely." So soft. Such a gentle picture. I passed the tablet back. "But you didn't sign it. You should sign it." I could tell he didn't want to, that a signature meant he was taking himself too seriously. "Please."

He signed his name in the corner, very small and discreet, then passed it back.

"I'll frame it."

His face fell. "Don't do that."

"Why not? I'd love to put it on the wall."

"No. It's not good enough. I've never framed any of my drawings. I don't want them framed."

"Okay." But I would do something special with it. I wasn't yet sure what. In the bedroom, we undressed.

I think he'd been ready for me most of the evening, but now that we'd moved past the drawing, he'd reached a point where polite restraint was done and over.

His hands were on the gown.

"Don't tear it." I couldn't bear to have the vintage fabric torn.

He paused long enough for me to pull it over my head, and then we tumbled to the mattress, his sudden passion at odds with the cool and collected artist of minutes ago. And it was his left hand that caressed my breast. And it was his left hand that slipped between my thighs.

"I thought you'd vanished tonight," he said. "I came home and you weren't here. I thought you'd left. And then your car was gone, and the police called." His voice caught. His weight pinned me to the bed, heavy and solid and alive. "They wouldn't tell me anything over the phone, and when I saw the car...the blood on the road...I thought you were dead."

I parted my legs for him, while at the same time wondering why I'd ever been upset enough to leave.

Don't think. Just don't think and everything will be fine. Everything will be wonderful.

Adrian's world wasn't a place for thinking.

I'm not sure if it was lovemaking as much as it was Adrian's need to get as close to me as he could, as if the physical act would somehow make up for a bond that didn't yet exist and maybe never would exist between us. And I have to admit that when he touched me I lost track of who he was and who I was. We were just two people, two bodies coming together in the dark.

And in that dark, maybe I *was* someone else.

An hour later, I could feel his thoughtful silence in the dark beside me, and I sensed that he was mulling something over in his head. Finally he spoke, and when he did, his words proved I wasn't being paranoid.

"I almost didn't go through with the marriage," he confessed. "My parents and brother tried to talk me out of it right up until the last minute. They came close to convincing me I was making a mistake." He pulled in a deep breath, then exhaled. "That night, after we were married, when I left to check the trees, I stopped at the farmhouse. I was upset, having second thoughts, and my parents assured me we could have the marriage annulled."

"So you went drinking."

"Yeah."

"Why didn't you tell me? Why didn't you come back here and talk to me?"

"I was trying to sort it out in my head. Talking to you, seeing you, would have confused me more."

So I was left to pick up on an underlying, unearned resentment and the feeling that I'd done something wrong while he continued to live an odd, dual existence: the one he couldn't leave behind, the son, the child, and that of a married man with a wife.

"My mother thinks you tricked me into marrying you, and I started wondering if maybe she was right."

"Getting married was your idea." Had he so quickly forgotten? "I suggested living together."

"I know, but I started questioning everything, wondering if I'd been manipulated somehow."

The naïve country boy manipulated by the slick city girl. This was a role I couldn't tolerate. I tossed back the covers with the intention of finding my clothes. I would walk if I couldn't drive. I would hitchhike.

He grabbed my arm. Just enough to stop me, his fingers trailing away.

"Come on. I'm being honest with you. That's what you wanted, wasn't it?"

I was beginning to grasp the full extent of the sheltered and isolated life he'd led, hardly ever leaving the orchard, having very little contact with people beyond the farm. His social skills were undeveloped, but maybe I was making excuses for him. His charm was rooted in the fact that he was unlike anybody I'd ever met, and much of that came from his lack of influence by the outside world.

I could now see that everybody had been right about our being a poor match and being too young, but I was stubborn. I found myself wanting to prove them wrong.

CHAPTER NINETEEN

Albuquerque, New Mexico, 1968

I was twelve and my younger brother six the year Robert Kennedy was assassinated. We still lived in Albuquerque. Not the Valley any longer, but a nondescript area of the Heights, part of the sprawl that would soon reach the Sandia Mountains.

My mother was disposing of us one at a time, and my older brother had been shipped back to Burlington to live with our grandmother. A man named Freddy Fontaine had become a permanent fixture in our lives. He'd moved from France as a child and was now a United States CIA agent, information he eventually shared with my mother with the request that she not tell anyone. He cared about her deeply and didn't want her to get hurt.

Like any decent secret agent, Freddy had a lot of handguns, and we spent Saturday afternoons in the foothills shooting cans from rocks, going through boxes of bullets. His guns had intriguing names like Colt and Ruger. Some were revolvers, and some came with clips that Freddy loaded and clicked into place with professional efficiency. I preferred his rifles because I could steady the butt against my shoulder for better aim. Freddy praised my skill.

My younger brother was enthralled with the idea of his mother dating a secret agent. A man with a badge. A man with guns. A man with a cool car, complete with a siren and bullhorn. There was nothing we loved more than riding around in the backseat of Freddy's big red-and-white convertible.

The man fed us well, and under Freddy's care we thrived and put on weight. But the meals came with a price. Freddy loved nothing more than causing public scenes, roaring with laughter at everyone's discomfort. He was loud and demanding, only happy when he was making some poor waitress miserable, and only happy when everyone in the restaurant was looking at him. Often the manager had to be called to our table.

"Do you know who I am?" Freddy would flash his badge, careful to reveal the gun he always carried in a holster under his jacket. The manager would become apologetic, and we would end up with free drinks and free food.

I could have almost understood my mother's devotion if Freddy had been some dreamboat, but he was fat, short, ugly, and obnoxious. But he adored her, and she needed to be adored. "Being a CIA agent is very stressful work," she told us, making excuses for his juvenile behavior.

"I don't know what his job has to do with anything," I said.

"The way he acts—it's a release valve. He's under a tremendous amount of pressure," she said. "He's told me some things he has to deal with, things I can't tell anyone, not even you two."

They would drop me and my brother off at the movie theater, and when they returned to pick us up, long after the movie ended, they were usually drunk, my mother's lipstick smeared and her clothes in disarray, both of them giggling and hanging on each other. He would massage her breasts in front of us, and she would smile. It was always a relief to see her happy, no matter the circumstances and no matter that I knew the happiness wouldn't last.

One day at a grocery store, a man waved and shouted to Freddy from the opposite end of the dairy section. "Frederico! What are you doing in this part of town?"

"You must be confusing me with someone else." Freddy gave the man a hard stare, as if trying to transmit some secret information. But his friend didn't seem to get it and, with a look of confusion, said, "See you at the shop on Monday."

"Shop?" my mother asked.

"It's a cover," Freddy said. "It has to do with my job."

She nodded, understanding.

But finally my mother found out the truth about her CIA agent. His real name was Frederico Florez, and he was a car mechanic.

A week after she dumped him, he pounded on our front door. "Let me in! I have a gun!"

It was late evening, and my brother and I were by ourselves. We crouched down, away from the front window. "Leave us alone!" I shouted over the television and *Star Trek*. "She's not here!" Going for the phone and possible help would have meant walking in front of the kitchen window. I didn't dare try it.

"I'm getting a screwdriver!" His words were slurred, and I hoped he was too drunk to follow through on his plan, whatever it was. I heard him stumbling around, crashing through shrubbery. A car trunk slammed; then he was back, working at the door handle.

"Let me in or I'll call the cops!" he shouted.

My brother and I both laughed, Freddy's words a comforting reminder of his foolishness. Maybe he was no real threat. Finally the noise at the front door stopped. A few minutes later, I heard him trying to force open a bedroom window, scratching and cursing like some crazy cat in heat. While he was occupied at the back of the house, I ran for the phone and dialed the police.

Freddy was nowhere around when they arrived, but he'd left gouges on the front door where he'd tried to force it open, proof that he'd been there.

"At least he didn't do any real damage," my mother said when she returned home from her date. She wasn't overly concerned. But the next morning she went outside to get her clothes from the line and discovered that her best bras and panties were gone.

"Bali bras are expensive," she said forlornly.

I didn't understand why Freddy would want bras and panties, and I kept trying to imagine what he'd do with them. Throw them from the window one at a time while his car hurtled down the freeway? Spread them on his bed? Put them on and dance around his living room? Hang a bra from the rearview mirror of his convertible? For some reason that seemed the most likely outcome, and I almost wished I could see it.

Did it matter? He was gone. And hopefully he wasn't coming back. But I knew it meant another guy was just around the corner.

CHAPTER TWENTY

The day after the car wreck and Adrian's confession, I decided to visit Connie. When I stepped off Curtis land, the terrain returned to what was typical of the area—flat ground and unbroken fields that went on forever. Nothing relieved by hills or ravines too steep to plant. If a tractor could pull a plow without tipping over, the ground was farmed. Ditch to ditch, field to field, every inch was utilized. In summer, a person could forget about the marks left by the plow blade, forget about the barren winter when black earth contrasted with lines of white snow. Where, even now after a rain, arrowheads could be found glinting in the sunlight. In summer, when the corn grew ten feet tall, you could forget about the miles and acres that lay bare, exposed, and unprotected the rest of the year.

A mile or more in the distance, I spotted undefined shapes of green tractors pulling sprayers across fields, heat from the soil creating a mirage so the vehicles appeared to hover above the shimmering and shifting ground.

Soybeans brushed my ankles. I've never been a fan of soybeans. Corn seemed much more alive. It put off heat, and that wonderful humid aroma that was greener than any grass. Soybeans just sat there, kind of a pathetic apology. I felt bad that I didn't like them, but I couldn't help it.

Maybe I knew too much about soybeans, knew they required more chemicals to farm. Chemicals were even used to kill the soybean plant before harvest because the pulpy, spindly, stringy leaves and stems would otherwise plug up a combine after just one sweep. So when I looked at soybeans, I got the idea they were trying to appear cute and harmless, when really they were one giant Superfund site.

And yet my heart still responded to nature even when that nature was no longer natural. Even when it had been forced into straight lines and miles of the same, because there was an incredible beauty in symmetry and control on such a massive scale.

Modern farmers were artists, destructive architects of the land. And I could still appreciate the red-winged blackbirds that watched me from the furrowed fields, and the hot wind that blew across acres stripped bare. Birds still sang the same song, even though their habitat was forever changed, even though the trees and prairie grass were gone, never to return.

Fifteen minutes into my walk, I noticed a fine layer of dirt on my arms—a soft dusting of powder that was a combination of topsoil, fertilizer, and herbicide.

I'd heard topsoil could travel across entire states. It touched down in rivers and streams to be carried all the way to the Gulf. I didn't know if it was true, but it made sense. Someone once told me that nobody really cared what happened in the Midwest, that nobody really cared about all the pesticide and herbicide, but I had to wonder what people would think if they could stand here where I was standing. If they could breathe and feel and taste this air.

I found the metal sign Connie had mentioned. An advertisement for DeKalb corn. Not sure what purpose it served nailed to a fencepost in the middle of nowhere, but there it was. In the distance I spotted a grouping of trees that indicated a house. I turned and headed toward it.

The cornfield and lane ended at the edge of a large, sweeping backyard. A garden. Fruit trees. Clothesline with sheets and towels.

A border collie erupted out of nowhere and shot across the yard toward me, barking, tail wagging. I let the dog sniff me, and when it appeared it wasn't going to bite, I lowered my hand and let it investigate more thoroughly before I chanced a pat on the head. It seemed to like that, so hopefully we were okay. I didn't know a lot about dogs, but it looked like it was smiling, happy to have company as it trotted beside me.

The building was a typical rural farmhouse. Two stories tall, with a big front porch supported by wooden posts painted white like the rest of the structure. It sat on a slightly elevated piece of ground, the front yard shaded by a giant oak with a twisted trunk. The property was located at the end of a lane and felt private, remote, and peaceful.

Across the gravel drive stood a corncrib in various stages of decay, with more gray wood than white. Window frames clung to broken, opaque glass that had once been clear.

The dog continued to bark and circle me, acting like a puppy even though it was gray around the mouth and eyes. A screen door slammed, and Connie stepped onto the porch. "Come here, Sophie. Here, girl."

The dog struggled between continuing to visit with me and doing what she was told. Connie gave her a sharper command, and Sophie turned and ran to the porch.

"She doesn't mind very well," Connie said as if my visit weren't the least unusual, or as if she'd just seen me five minutes ago. She straightened, raised both arms, and tightened the ponytail on the back of her head. "I was getting ready to have some iced tea. Come in and join me."

I thought she was actually glad to see me, but I couldn't be sure about that. I followed her inside.

Connie walked to the sink, turned on the water, and began washing her hands. "I've been cultivating corn all morning." She spoke over her shoulder, water splashing. "Forgot my thermos, so I left the tractor in the field and walked back."

"I don't want to interrupt anything," I said.

"You aren't." She dried her hands on a red-and-white cotton towel, then tossed it on the counter. "Perfect timing. I could use a little company. The radio on the tractor doesn't work, and I'm sick of being stuck with my own thoughts."

She opened the freezer, pulled out a container of ice cubes, filled two glasses, then poured tea from a plastic pitcher. "You take sugar?"

"No." I stepped closer to the wall to examine a cluster of framed photos. One image was of a young Connie and a middle-aged couple posing in front of a colonial-style house. No leaves on the trees, but the grass was green so it must have been early spring. They were dressed up, and I had the feeling it could have been Easter.

The older woman was pregnant.

"That's my mother. She miscarried the day after that photo was taken. It was her fifth miscarriage in two years."

"How awful."

"There were a lot of miscarriages around here during that period. I blame it on drift from the fields, but we don't point fingers. Every occupation has its hazards."

"That's more than an occupational hazard." I was surprised by Connie's complacency. "I think people get used to life being a certain way," I said. "They accept things they shouldn't accept."

"You have no right to judge us."

Her defensive reply took me by surprise, yet at the same time, I knew what she meant. I could sense a twisted tangle of complexities that were tied to farming and generations and tradition, things an outsider like me would never be able to fully grasp. But it still hurt for her to point out that I wasn't one of them.

She got up and made a big production of turning on the box fan in the corner and arranging it so it blew toward the table; then she sat back down. The noise took away some of the awkwardness.

"What in the world happened to your head?" She leaned forward and touched the ugly lump. It was already turning yellow around the edges. I'd tried to hide it, but my cropped hair was too short.

I told her about the wreck. And I told her about Adrian continuing to eat with his parents. But just that morning he'd brought armloads of clothes to our house, taking a step toward truly moving in, the public shift of belongings a statement to everyone on the farm.

"Good God." She tipped her head and pressed her lips together in a sad smile. "Do you care about him so much? Do you love him?"

My face must have reflected more than I myself understood, because her look of sympathy increased. "Do you know his mother tied his hand to his side to force him to become right-handed?" I asked.

"Doesn't surprise me. The Curtis farm is all about perfection. Perfect apples, perfect corn, perfect people, perfect life. Nothing flawed can exist there. But you also have to realize people around here are superstitious. They still believe a lot of old folklore."

Connie and I were on the same side again. "His mother seems driven by fear," I said. "Fear of being different." For someone like me, someone who'd never wanted to be like anybody else, I couldn't fathom that way of thinking, even when I recognized the reasoning behind it.

The dog scratched at the door, and Connie let her in. She immediately ran to me, tail wagging. The ticking of the plastic clock on the wall seemed to grow louder, and suddenly the dog looked as if she had a secret.

I finished my tea and got up to leave.

"Would you like a ride home?"

"Thanks. I can walk."

"Let me give you a lift. I need to run to town anyway, and it's getting hot out."

We rode back to the Curtis farm in her truck, and when we pulled into the grass-and-gravel drive, Adrian stepped off the porch and strode toward us. At first his expression was anxious, and I realized he thought I'd run off again. Connie cut the engine and we both exited the truck, doors slamming.

"In the field today?" Connie asked, glancing at the orange-and-tan David Brown tractor parked along the road.

"Mowing hay," Adrian said. "You?"

"Cultivating corn. Kind of wishing I'd gone no-till this year."

"I don't know," Adrian said. "Too risky and expensive. Chemicals have to be applied at the right time. And if it rains too much or rains too little you might end up cultivating anyway."

Connie nodded while I stood on the edge of their conversation, unable to participate. Connie was attractive. Smart. A hard worker. Her farm was nearby. She was part of Adrian's world. If I'd been a matchmaker, I would have paired them off. I would never have chosen me. Not in a million years.

"Maybe I could learn to plow," I said after Connie left and Adrian was heading for the David Brown tractor.

He swung back around, an odd expression on his face.

"Or I could mow pasture," I offered.

"Women don't drive tractors here."

I laughed. I thought he was kidding.

"Really. I mean, I know you could learn to drive a tractor. And I know you could mow pasture, but on this farm women aren't allowed to drive tractors. It's a man's job."

"You mean your mother has never driven a tractor?"

"No."

"Could she drive one if she had to?"

"I'm not sure. I don't think so."

"And she's okay with that?"

"It's her rule."

I laughed again. Of course it was. The decree was ridiculous, but I had to wonder if it was less about sexism and more about a way to efficiently distribute the workload. And who was I to question the cultural male/female boundaries established long before I showed up?

"Do your man thing, and I'll go in the house and do my woman thing." I was making fun of their silly rules, but at the same time I felt the pull of housekeeping and cooking. I thought about what I might prepare for dinner, and I thought about painting the kitchen a lovely pale yellow. These things would occupy my time and keep me content for a while, and a while was all I needed to think about.

CHAPTER TWENTY-ONE

A few days after my visit with Connie, the phone rang. At first I couldn't figure out who was calling or what the woman wanted. I finally realized the voice at the other end of the line belonged to my grandmother's sister. Because of the divorce, I didn't know my grandmother's relatives well, but over the years I'd spent a few Sunday afternoons at her sister's house.

"Your grandmother had a stroke." The sister sounded as if she'd been crying. "She's in the hospital and isn't expected to live another hour. You have to get here fast."

I couldn't find Adrian, but I found his truck, the keys in the ignition. I drove off, part of me anxious to get away without being stopped, the other fearful of arriving at my destination.

Twelve miles.

That's how far it was from the farm to the hospital. I took the rickety bridge across the Mississippi. The water made me think of my grandmother. We hadn't been river rats, but when you spent years on the banks of the Mississippi River, it became a part of you in ways you didn't understand. I imagined my grandmother's soul being swept away by the current to pause briefly and snag on an eddy, then move downstream.

At the hospital, I drove in circles until I finally forced myself to pull into a parking spot. Inside, I found an information desk and choked out my question and my grandmother's name. It took the receptionist a few minutes to determine that she was in intensive care. She told me where to go, and I tried to follow her directions, winding around the hospital to end in a dark hallway that seemed like a basement.

I spotted my grandmother's relatives, and from their faces I knew I was too late. She was dead at seventy-two. I had known when I crossed the bridge.

"Do you want to see her?" someone asked.

It took me a moment to realize they were asking if I wanted to see the body. I pressed my lips together and shook my head. Someone hugged me.

I couldn't stand to stay there any longer. I turned and left, hurrying back to the truck.

Drive.

Just drive.

I drove where I usually drove when things were bad.

To her house.

I parked in the alley and dug in my bag for the skeleton key I always carried.

Keeping my head down, hoping none of the neighbors would appear to ask how she was, I unlocked the back door, stepped inside, and locked it behind me.

I stared at my shaking hands. I wanted to tell someone, but she was the one I would have told. She was the one I would have called.

I walked to the buffet and looked for the tapered candle she'd shown me several times. There it was. Light blue. Faded. On it was a wedding band she'd quit wearing when her knuckles had gotten too big.

"When I die, make sure they bury me with my ring."

"Don't talk about dying," I'd told her.

I'd given her the assurance she'd wanted, while inside I'd told myself I'd never need to see it through. But still, I'd promised.

I wandered through the house. There was her bed. Her chair. Her hairbrush and hand mirror. In the bathroom was the toilet seat my father had given her for Christmas. Who gives someone a toilet seat? But she'd been thrilled. It was soft, and when her friends came over, she'd take them into the bathroom and show it to them.

"He gave it to me for Christmas," she'd say with pride. They would poke it and laugh.

CHAPTER TWENTY-TWO

I hadn't planned to return to my grandmother's house, but two days later I remembered the ring and drove back to Burlington. I ran up steps I'd climbed ever since I could walk. Through the kitchen that still smelled like ironed cotton sheets, to the dining room and the buffet.

"Where's the ring?"

Blank faces of my grandmother's sisters.

"Her wedding ring." Someone must have taken it to the funeral home.

"I don't know anything about a ring," one of the women said.

Frantically I went through the house, asking each person I came upon.

Had it really been there two days ago? Was I just replaying old footage in my head? From the times my grandmother had told me about the ring? Or had I done something with it myself? In my grief, had I removed the ring from the candle and stuck it somewhere?

"The ring," I said. "She wanted to be buried with her wedding band."

Nobody knew what I was talking about.

Did it matter? Did it really matter? She was dead.

Had someone taken the ring? Who? It hadn't been very big. Not a wide gold band. It couldn't have been worth much. I kept staring at the blue tapered candle, thinking the ring would appear.

If something could vanish, it could come back.

"You'll help me paint the house this spring, won't you?" she'd asked me. I'd promised to do that too, and now it wasn't going to happen.

I went into the spare bedroom, shut the door, and sat down on the bed. The mattress was indented in two places and had been moved from the main bedroom when it had gotten old. Two troughs made by two people who no longer existed. This was my room. I'd stayed in it a lot. Sometimes for a day, sometimes for weeks.

"You always have a place here. You can always come here."

And I had. Come knocking in the middle of the night. Broke, dirty, hungry.

Somewhere in the back of my mind, I got the sense that my marriage had opened a door, and now this avalanche of bad was pouring in.

I looked in the closet. One of my suitcases was still there, along with some of my things. I put the suitcase on the bed and began filling it.

I sensed Adrian's shadowy presence on the edge of my grief, but he didn't say anything to me about my grandmother. Not a word. Not a touch that might have conveyed a hint of sympathy. His parents offered hollow condolences that were nothing more than social obligation, but I was too numb to care.

Days later, when I reran the funeral in my head, I had little memory of Adrian at the church or at the family gathering at my grandmother's house, but I knew he'd been there.

It was comforting to know I'd lost hours.

She was gone. The ring was gone.

That was real.

But it wasn't something I could grasp. And I didn't want to grasp it, because I wanted to hold on to her a little longer.

CHAPTER TWENTY-THREE

Her life was strewn across the backyard, and strangers pawed through it.

At first I'd flat-out refused to go to the auction. I wouldn't be a part of such grave robbing and disrespect. But in the end, I couldn't stay away. Partially because I couldn't believe it was happening. I thought I might have misunderstood the extent of the plan. But standing there on the edge of the crowd, the auctioneer bellowing in the microphone, I knew I hadn't. I had to quit giving people breaks. I had to quit expecting more out of them than they would ever give.

The long tables of beautifully crocheted masterpieces hurt the most.

Symbols of her life. Of time and years and evenings spent on the back porch waiting for the house to cool. Hands and thread, creating loveliness from nothing. So personal. They'd never asked me if I wanted any of it. I was handed three handkerchiefs. "We thought you might like these," my dad's wife said, as if bestowing some generous gift on me. As if she had any right to bestow.

My grandmother's life had been reduced to trash. Some inconvenience to be dealt with as quickly as possible. Auctions were for people with no family. You didn't auction off your mother's belongings. You didn't spread it out on the lawn for the whole world to see what you didn't cherish.

The house was also being sold, the event orchestrated by my father and his wife. *Let's just get rid of all this crap at the same time. Drive up and do it in an afternoon. Take the money and run.*

For thirteen years, ever since Florida, my dad and Eve had lived together rather than marry in order for her to continue receiving a lavish alimony check. But her ex-husband had recently died, the funds had stopped, and she and my father had finally tied the knot. I'd run into them a handful of times over the years, and the encounters were always awkward and uncomfortable.

Now I watched from the sidelines as crocheted tablecloths sold for pennies. Each piece had taken months to create; each piece represented a moment in a life. I should have bid on them myself. I would regret it in the future, but I was so hurt and so mad that I simply refused to be a part of it.

Yet here I stood.

Watching.

I'd come because I'd hoped they would have second thoughts about the crocheted and embroidered things. I'd secretly hoped they'd put aside at least some of them for me. Surely they were selling only the more common pieces. Because it was unfathomable to me that someone would put such symbols of a person's life in an auction unless the deceased was someone you didn't know. Unless the deceased had no family.

But there were no linens for me. None for my grandmother's sisters and brothers, either, who would have cherished them. I saw some of them in the crowd and saw my own numb disbelief in their eyes.

A vendor sold hot dogs and popcorn. People were milling about like it was some carnival. At one point, I went inside to use the bathroom.

The toilet seat hadn't been removed. I was a little surprised that my father hadn't put it in his car to take home, or put it in the auction. I was heading back outside when I found Eve sobbing in the middle of the living room.

She and my grandmother hadn't been even remotely close, probably because they'd been the same age. That kind of thing could create an awkward barrier. I was touched and surprised to see the tears. Maybe

I'd misjudged her. I started crying a little myself, which made her tears increase. Pretty soon we were hugging each other, but just for a second before breaking away, as if both realizing touching had been a mistake and we'd taken things too far.

"Oh, it's awful. Just awful," she said once she got her sobbing under control.

"I know." I started to whimper again. Here was someone who could understand my pain. Even just a little.

She looked at me, and in her eyes I could see that connection of shared misery and heartache. "It sold for nothing."

She lost me. "What are you talking about?"

She dabbed at her eyes. "The television! The color television! It sold for fifteen dollars!" She broke down again with a fresh round of sobs.

The woman who hadn't shed a tear up to that point was crying over a color television. And I now suspected she was behind the disappearance of the wedding ring.

I walked back outside.

I should have left the auction, but I had to see the house sell. I thought about the key in my bag, a key that would unlock the door to a house that would soon hold strangers. I wouldn't give it back. Nobody knew I had it. It would always be my grandmother's house no matter how many years passed or how many strangers owned it.

I don't know how much Eve expected to get for the property, but I watched her face as the auction progressed, and I could see another tear fest in the making.

The house my grandmother and grandfather had built with their own hands ended up selling for almost nothing.

I should have tried to somehow buy it, maybe get a loan, but at twenty-one you don't think about such things. Eve vanished, and I imagined her in the living room, sobbing her dark heart out.

I covertly watched the new owners. A young couple. Someone said they were newlyweds. She was blond. He had dark hair. They were happy that day.

Nobody would have guessed that a year later the guy would blow his brains out in my grandmother's basement.

CHAPTER TWENTY-FOUR

Parked in the driveway was an unfamiliar truck with a small white trailer attached. My new husband and two men stood in the yard with a horse. A young red thing with a shiny sleek coat, smooth muscles, and four black hooves. I stepped outside and immediately smelled the animal. Skin and sweat and hair.

One of the men broke away and took a few steps in my direction. "I'm sorry about your grandmother."

Adrian saw my confusion. "The horse is for you."

"You bought me a horse?" I felt a spark of life, but also disbelief and irritation. I mean, what the hell? A horse? My grandmother had been dead two weeks, and in that time Adrian had never offered a word of sympathy, yet he went out and bought me a horse?

I moved closer, and the horse got fidgety and nervous. "It's not broken?"

"No," one of the traders said. "But it won't take long." To demonstrate the animal's gentle nature, he draped himself over its back. The horse tolerated the weight. The guy got brave and swung a leg over, and the rodeo began. Within two seconds the man was on the ground. Everybody laughed.

They reloaded the horse into the trailer and drove it to a small pen near the corncrib, where Adrian could keep a close eye on it. I returned to the house, baffled by his actions.

The next day Adrian blustered in. "I've got a saddle and halter on her. She doesn't seem to mind it. No bucking at all. She's going to be a mellow thing." This was the most animated and communicative Adrian had been since the night I'd tried to leave.

I climbed in the passenger seat of the truck, and we headed for the crib. Halfway there, Adrian tensed. The pickup shot forward and we flew down the road, turned into the crib lane, and pulled to a dusty stop in front of a set of pens. Adrian bailed out, vaulted over a fence. I followed and reached the gate in time to see the glint of a pocketknife.

The horse was hanging by the halter, tongue lolling to the side of a foamed mouth. Eyes blank.

Adrian sliced the tie rope and the horse hit the ground with a rolling thud. Without pause, he began kicking the dead animal, hoping to make it take a breath.

The strangulation of the horse was bad enough, but the violent scene playing out in front of me lifted a sad tragedy to another level of awful. Panting, legs spread over the carcass, Adrian finally looked up at me.

The horror I felt must have shown on my face. He was hard to read, but I could see the moment it occurred to him how enormously his gift had backfired, how it had gone from something that might make me feel better to something that could only compound my grief.

And yet in that odd, horrible moment, I at last understood that Adrian was unable to communicate his emotions verbally and the horse had been his way of telling me he was sorry about my grandmother.

The Family

CHAPTER TWENTY-FIVE

The skin of the early summer apple is thin, almost translucent, and the flesh is white. I was picking a variety called Transparent. Adrian's great-grandfather had planted two rows, but this broken, gnarled tree was the only one left. The rest had been bulldozed to make room for easier-to-pick dwarf trees.

I'd started early. Two hours later, the dew still clung to orchard grass, and a haze still hovered above distant cornfields. I stood high on a wooden ladder that was wide at the bottom and narrow at the top. The thick straps of the picking basket pressed into my shoulders as I filled the metal container that rested against my belly like a baby carrier. It was an ingenious and simple way to pick, leaving both hands free.

When the apples reached the rim of the container, I climbed down the ladder, unhooked the two sections of cotton rope from the picking basket, releasing the red canvas sleeve at the bottom, allowing the apples to roll into the wooden crates that waited in the grass near the base of the tree. Once the basket was empty, I wound the sections of rope over the hooks, securing the sleeve once more.

Picking had been Adrian's idea. I was still grieving, and it felt good to get out of the house, felt good to be doing physical labor. My grandmother's death had brought about another small measure of change, and Adrian seemed to recognize our marriage as something to value. He was no longer eating dinner with his parents, and despite our undefined relationship, Adrian, this newcomer to my life, was now the only close family I had. Such an odd thing to think about.

I shed my sweatshirt, tossing it to the grass from my perch high on the ladder. Adrian's mother had been skeptical about my picking, and she'd even stood at the base of the tree to make sure I did it correctly.

"Twist and pull," she'd instructed. "Nobody wants apples with no stems. And don't grasp them too firmly. Your fingers will leave bruises."

She'd been right about that. The first bushel was doomed to end up as seconds because my fingerprints appeared an hour after picking, but now I was finally getting the hang of it.

I twisted and pulled but occasionally still produced an apple with no stem. I rubbed a stemless apple on the leg of my jeans as if I could wipe off the toxins. But an agent was added to the chemicals to make them adhere to the surface of the apple, and no amount of rubbing and scrubbing could remove it all. And an apple like this—a Transparent—how much pesticide leached through?

I took a bite. The thin skin made a crisp, snapping sound, and my mouth filled with sour juice. Not your ideal eating apple. Most of the older locals used them for applesauce, adding a lot of sugar.

I finished the apple and tossed the core, thinking about how the seeds wouldn't grow a Transparent apple tree. That seemed crazy and mysterious to me.

The apples were so thick they weighed down the branches, which cascaded to the ground. I moved the ladder to another spot, climbing higher to reach a cluster of fruit near the top. From this vantage point, I saw cars driving down the highway, and I could see ribbons of roads winding through green fields. Pastures dotted with Black Angus cattle. Nearer, on Curtis land, I spotted what looked like the knoll with the pioneer grave Adrian had shown me that perfect day. I studied the terrain, searching for the tiny cabin in the woods. The foliage was too dense, but I spotted a cluster of trees that might have been the location. Nearby was the sagging wooden gate with the little metal sign advertising tobacco. There was the pasture, and beside it, dark timber and steep ravines. Familiar, but different because it was now overgrown. Different because I was different.

A death. A loss.

Somewhere far away, a tractor moved through a field, and I vaguely recalled Adrian saying something about mowing hay. The sound of the diesel engine reminded me that I wasn't completely alone, but it also reminded me that what Adrian and I shared might never be real.

It began to rain, and at first the cold drops felt good on my face, but soon they began to sting. I climbed down the ladder, dumped the load of apples, and ducked out of the harness. I stood under the protection of an apple tree, listening to the patter on the leaves above me. The sound was unbelievably sad, but all sounds were sad now, even the call of birds. I gradually became aware of a tempo change, and a hollow patter that was closer than the leaves above my head. I turned to see one of the red paper boxes used to monitor moths just beyond my shoulder. The little tent was full.

I wiped the back of my hand across my mouth, tasting the pesticide being washed from the leaves. Adrian and his father kept spraying, but the moths still came.

CHAPTER TWENTY-SIX

New Mexico, 1969–1972

I was thirteen when my mother met David, a man who'd spent most of his life in a strict religious environment. At age twelve, David had been sent to live at a monastery run by the Christian Brothers. Twenty-five years later, just weeks before taking his final vows to become a brother himself, he decided he wanted to find out what he was missing. He wanted to know what it was like to have a girlfriend, have a wife, have a family. In a vulnerable state and as randy as a teenager, he ran into my mother.

In order to be alone, they spent evenings at drive-ins, then came home drunk, tumbling into bed, leaving the door wide open to the same room where my mother and Freddy had frolicked.

"We're both going to confession today," my mother would tell me the next morning. This was delivered with a wicked giggle. I wasn't sure if they'd actually had sex, or if it had been what my mother called "heavy petting."

He never stayed the entire night. That would have been inappropriate, but he would swing by early the next morning, a box of donuts in his hand. Later, they went to confession and the whole thing would start again.

I wasn't invested in the new guy, and I knew if I bided my time he would soon be gone. Oddly enough, I was happy. I'd found my groove, and I knew these guys didn't mean anything. They weren't important. In fact, they were my entertainment. They added something to my life, my own up-close-and-personal study of dating and relationships. And my mother's secretarial job, combined with her obsessive involvement with men and dating, left me free to do whatever I wanted as long as I kept one eye on my younger brother. Stay up all night listening to the radio if I felt like it. Skip school if I felt like it. Eat whatever I wanted, whenever I wanted. Take a bath, not take a bath. Never wash my sheets, read all day long while drinking pop and eating candy. I was as content as a cat. No expectations, no pressure.

But David stuck around.

"Let me take your picture," he told me one day. "I want photos of all of you so I can show them to my coworkers."

I crossed my arms over my chest, refusing. None of the boyfriends had ever taken pictures of us.

"Come on," my mother coaxed. It was late afternoon. I'd just returned from school and we were standing in the front yard. I could smell the marigolds that ran along the walk, and I could feel winter coming.

"Let David take your picture."

He took the photo with a Polaroid camera, and once it developed he handed it to me. My mother hated Polaroid cameras. She said they took horrible pictures and were a foolish waste of money. I wondered if I should tell him that.

And there I was, in my short purple-and-green-striped dress and fringed leather knee boots, in front of a house made of cement block— one story with a flat roof and ugly crank windows. My hair was long and straightened, parted in the center. My arms were crossed defiantly, a hip jutting out, the expression on my face one of loathing.

I was surprised to see my emotions so evident. I felt bad and handed the picture back to him. "That's nice," I mumbled. He was the first real dork I'd ever known, certainly the first one my mother had brought home.

"I'm going to put it on my desk," he said with a big smile, tucking the photo into his shirt pocket. He was a math professor at a new college in a little desert town in southern New Mexico. I'd gotten the scoop: the College of Artesia was a party school, known for accepting anybody, no matter the grades. Rich parents sent their spoiled brats there, and the school was also a popular place for people who wanted to avoid the Vietnam draft.

It wasn't that I hated every guy my mother dated. That wasn't it. I hated the ones who were so obviously wrong for her. Wrong for *us*. I'd adored the shy painter who'd been madly in love with her. I'd wanted him to be a part of our family, and I was heartbroken when she dumped him. I'd liked the twin brothers who'd both had a crush on her. I didn't resent all the men in her life, only the ones who weren't worthy of us.

My mother didn't love David. I was pretty sure of that. She hadn't loved any of them. They were her do-overs.

We made a few trips from Albuquerque to Artesia, and pretty soon there was talk of getting married, and pretty soon they'd bought a house, and pretty soon we moved to the middle of nowhere, and my younger brother and I were once again starting a new school.

People in Artesia had exaggerated southern accents, and everybody sounded as if they were in a bad high school play. Girls at the public junior high school wore saddle shoes and skirts that fell to their knees, and for lunch they dumped small packets of salted peanuts into a bottle of Pepsi, put their thumbs over the glass lip, and gave it a good shake. They said *y'all* and *ma'am* and told me I sounded like someone from television. Within a few months I was saying *y'all* and *ma'am* and dumping peanuts in my Pepsi. But I refused to wear skirts that fell to my knees.

David was malleable. He could be anyone my mother wanted him to be, and he would do whatever she said, no questions asked. If she told him to beat me, he would do it with no expression on his face. If she told him to lock me out of the house, he did. Sometimes I thought he might be the epitome of evil, and at other times I felt sorry for him and saw him as a helpless victim. He didn't have a chance against her, but I don't know if that was any excuse for his weakness.

My mother didn't think of me as her daughter, but rather a person who'd had a hand in ruining her life. "You look like him," she would tell me with confusion and hatred in her eyes, as if she'd gone back to Florida in her mind and was seeing the man who'd left us. She would never outrun that man. Deep down, my mother knew what a mess she'd made of her life, but there was no turning back. She was finally married. Her years of trying to correct and erase something that had happened in the past had led us to this new and bizarre existence.

A facade had been erected, not only for the people who looked at us from the outside, but for my mother and her new husband, and even for my younger brother. They'd gotten on this train, and they weren't getting off, and they would ride it out and pretend it was going somewhere nice. And sometimes it worked. ˙

My mother and the new husband and my younger brother made an odd family. My brother had never had a father, and he embraced the new life with gusto. He and his new parent did things together. My brother changed his last name, and he began to use the word *Dad*. He was too young to realize he was a traitor, not to the father he'd never known, but to our way of life. To our originality. He and his new father put together models, and the three of them took trips to the desert, returning with the treasures they'd collected. And sometimes I thought the new dad wasn't the person who didn't fit—*I* didn't fit.

Weekday mornings, David put on a gray suit and tie and pedaled his bicycle to school, as proud as a peacock, saddlebags bulging with the textbooks he'd strapped above the back tire, his posture straight, ringing the handlebar bell for no apparent reason, just to announce that he was happy. From the window of the school bus, kids would point and laugh. "Look at that weird guy! Oh my God. Look at him!" Students would rush to one side of the bus for a better view, laughing hysterically.

As the months ticked away, my mother's unhappiness increased. I began to dread stepping in the front door. My younger brother managed to stay beneath her radar, partly because he could charm his way out of anything, and partly because he was still thought of as the baby.

I would arrive home from school to find her in a rage, and that rage was usually directed at me. Maybe I'd forgotten to put a spoon in a special, designated cup in the sink. Maybe I'd used the wrong washcloth. The infractions were small, her behavior masking the real problem: she was miserable in her new life, and I was a reminder of the man who'd left her. She may have been able to fool my younger brother, but she couldn't fool me; I was old enough to see through her act and her pretense.

What are you doing? What have you done? My eyes asked the questions. This place, this man, were more wrong for her than the secret agent had been. Her days were filled with preparing meals, grocery shopping, cleaning house, nothing that remotely spoke of her. She was like a horse kept in a confined stall. Always volatile, she became even moodier and more unpredictable as she continued to force herself to wear the chafing skin of a housewife.

People thought my mother was clever and beautiful and artistic— bohemian cool—and few suspected what went on behind closed doors. A handful of friends witnessed the crazy stuff, the rages and the irrational behavior. Those friends never returned, and they quit associating with me. They would give me sideways glances in the school hall, or turn their backs and pretend to be concentrating on their lockers.

You learn to keep your mouth shut about such things.

The marriage made me long for the days of the revolving door, and the men who came and went. With them, I always knew the page would turn, and the guy would be gone and another would take his place. And for a brief time, my mother would be happy.

CHAPTER TWENTY-SEVEN

"I'm going to look for a job," I said.

It was evening, and Adrian and I sat on opposite ends of the couch, heads bent over sketch pads, me with a pencil and eraser, Adrian with pen and ink. Two months had passed since my grandmother's death. Every day was still tough, but the fog was lifting, and I occasionally caught myself laughing at something absurd or silly. Life held a hint of promise.

I preferred to sketch in scenes lightly with pencil, but I'd erased too much, and now the paper was beginning to show wear, and the people in the café scene were off. I was frustrated, which was often the case when it came to my drawings. For me, drawing was a struggle, and I sometimes wondered if I drew because people had always told me I should be an artist.

I swept eraser crumbs away with the back of my hand and tucked my feet farther under me. "Maybe something in Burlington."

I'd painted the kitchen yellow and hung yellow curtains in the windows above the porcelain sink. I'd refinished the living room floor and put down linoleum squares in the bathroom. I'd immersed myself in all things domestic as long as I could, until I began to understand how pioneer women lost their minds locked up in tiny cabins all day. And my grandmother had been right about the cooking wearing thin. I continued to concoct things I thought Adrian would enjoy, but so far nothing had impressed him.

He dipped his quill pen in the inkwell, careful to tap off the excess. That was followed by the sound of the sharp tip moving across rough paper. I'd already peeked and knew he was drawing a cowboy on a horse. He drew the most magnificent horses. "My mother is hiring part-time help," he said without looking up. "Apple baggers and sorters."

I tucked my pencil behind my ear, reached for a pack of cigarettes, and laughed out loud at the very idea of taking orders from his mom.

"No, really," he said. "You should work in the salesroom."

I didn't want to tell him his idea had disaster written all over it. Work for his mother?

"She has to hire somebody. It may as well be you. And then you wouldn't be driving back and forth in bad weather. Or in the dark."

And we both knew how good I was at that.

On the surface, working with apples should have been a perfectly logical solution, but I was quickly learning that nothing on the farm was logical.

He joined me for a smoke. "I'll talk to her." He shook out a match and tossed it in the ashtray. "I'll let her know you want to work for her."

Work *for* her. Not work for the farm. Not work *with* her. Work *for* her. But I also saw this as an opportunity to prove myself. To be a part of the farm. To be a part of Adrian's life. In fact, the more I thought about it, the more promising it seemed. "Okay." And really. What could be so hard about sorting apples and putting them in crates and bags?

I had little time to think about the foolishness of our idea. Early the next morning I headed out the door to work at my new place of employment under the critical eye of my mother-in-law. I wasn't lazy, and I'd done a stint at a Levi Strauss factory in Albuquerque, sewing pockets on jeans. I knew the drill of the tedious, and I understood the need for efficiency of movement and the contrasting skill of combining quality work with speed.

As I walked across the road to the salesroom, the rising sun hadn't yet warmed the air. Golden leaves from towering hickory trees drifted silently to the ground, softening my footfall. Dew dampened my leather boots, and I jammed my hands deep in the pockets of the hip-length sweater I'd picked up at a thrift store. The beauty of the morning raised my spirits, filling me with a sense of excitement and hope for the day and for my new adventure. Maybe this would work. Maybe this would even make everything okay.

As I circled the main house, I saw the view that greeted every visitor. A cluster of buildings, all painted a brilliant white. Adrian had told me the Victorian farmhouse with its gingerbread trim had once belonged to a preacher back when the farm was part of a small village, and wakes and viewings had been held in the parlor.

A circular drive with an entrance and exit. Two massive white barns and a long, low building that had once been a stable, carriage house, and blacksmith's shop but were now used mainly for storage. In the center of the parking area, an ancient windmill stood anchored to the ground, vines growing up the metal legs. A historical marker embedded in a rock reminded even the most casual visitor that this was a place of history, a place with a past that stretched back generations, the current occupants standing on the shoulders of the long dead.

The day was already under way, with pickups full of seasonal help heading down the road, the gravel still damp from dew and not yet making dust. Wearing a flannel shirt and jean jacket, Adrian waved to me from a tractor. He shifted gears. A puff of exhaust burst from the smokestack, and he took off toward the orchard pulling a flatbed loaded with crates.

Most everything that had to do with apples was done in a giant barn that had been expanded and converted into a salesroom, cider room, and sorting room. In the sorting room, apples rolled and bounced down conveyor belts to be ejected into areas designated by size, while women in sweatshirts, bandanas, and cotton gloves watched and removed damaged apples that would be either fed to cattle or made into cider. Music played on a small radio, and everybody seemed in a good mood but intent on their task. Sliding wooden doors big enough for full-size tractors stood open on both the east and west sides of the building, a cold and constant breeze blowing apple leaves to the cement floor. Pallets were stacked with wooden crates that towered above my head, the crates almost as old as the farm, CURTIS ORCHARD stenciled in black just below the handles. Inside, cold and sluggish bees clung to red fruit.

The crated apples were waiting to be inspected, or waiting to be taken to the coolers, or waiting to be bagged, or waiting to be made into cider. Somehow the placement in the barn defined their secret destiny, none of which made any sense to me.

I caught a brief glimpse of Adrian's father driving a forklift, moving pallets of apples from the main barn to the storage area in yet another white building. Our eyes met. His were blank, offering no welcome or acknowledgment. I got the distinct feeling my employment had been thoroughly discussed and given the stamp of disapproval. I found myself thinking that I had to do a good job, that I had to prove my worthiness to both of my in-laws. Then I quickly caught myself, realizing how pathetic my thoughts were. I didn't need to prove myself to anybody.

The smell of apples was so intense and so sweet it almost seemed artificial. It soaked into hair and clothes and skin, and when the women in front of the sorter smiled and waved in greeting, they somehow seemed a part of the soil and trees and fruit.

When the din couldn't seem to get any louder, someone opened the door to the cider room, where the high-pitched sound of apples being ground for the press caused alarmed children to scream and clap their hands to their ears.

Apples were best stored in temperatures a little above freezing. People dashed coatless from heated cars, plunging into the salesroom only to find the temperature no warmer within the closed doors. Inside they were quickly overwhelmed by variety. Apples for cooking, apples for eating, apples for pies, apples for applesauce. Apples that taste like wine, apples that taste like honey. Heirloom apples and new varieties.

I was put to work placing Golden Delicious in peck bags, one piece of fruit at a time, without bumping or dumping or rolling or dropping. I now knew that bruises wouldn't show up immediately, but in twenty-four hours a damaged apple would reveal imperfections.

At break time, everyone scattered. Some went to their cars, turned on the radio, popped open a soda, relaxed, and soaked in the solitude. Some wandered to the cider room and sampled the day's batch. Others stood in the open barn doors enjoying a smoke or eating a previously pocketed apple, saved for that very occasion.

I joined the smoking crowd—a combination of sorters and baggers.

"This your first day?" The question came from a big woman dressed in baggy jeans, light blue windbreaker, and floral scarf. Earlier I'd heard someone call her Georgia. She pulled a red apple from her pocket and took a bite. Her fingers were wrapped with black tape, and I'd already noticed that mine were sore from handling the cold fruit.

I nodded, wondering if I should explain who I was.

"My mother worked here," she told me. "And I started when I was sixteen." She continued her visual evaluation of me. "Ruth don't usually hire help like you."

I took a last drag from my cigarette, scraped it out on the ground, then tapped what remained back in my pack to save for later. "What do you mean?"

"She hires local."

"I'm local."

"Whose kid are you?"

I looked up from my cigarette pack to see Ruth glaring at me from across the parking lot.

"See what I mean?" Georgia said, noting the direction of my fixed stare. "You'd better not do any chatting while you work, and don't leave a second early. In fact, stay a half hour after your shift ends if you want to stick around here."

"Is she really so hard to get along with?" Ruth was now laughing and talking to a couple of white-haired women, all warmth and openness, helping them into their car with their jugs of cider. The two women were practically shining, gazing at her with admiration. And I suppose, in some ways, she might seem like royalty to them.

"Her son got married and she's had a bee in her bonnet ever since. We're all feeling the brunt of it, but she's a good woman. She really made something of herself."

"But she married into this place."

"She came from one of the poorest families in the county. Gobs of lazy, unemployed men living under one roof with their wives and babies. No running water, no electricity. Her daddy was crazy. Some said it was because of the war. I don't know. They all seemed a little off to me. But he didn't have a car or driver's license, and he used to drive to town on his riding mower, naked as a jaybird. But look at Mildred now."

"Mildred?"

"That's what we used to call her, but she changed everything about herself when she got married, even her first name. It's like she wanted to be a completely different person."

"How'd she meet Mr. Curtis?"

"A friend was doing bookwork for his daddy. Told Mildred Mr. Curtis had more money than he knew what to do with, and that pretty much started the wedding bells to chiming."

"That makes me feel a little sorry for her husband."

"You know he was with those other two kids when they died. Family vacation to Colorado. Three kids in the backseat. Two died from carbon monoxide poisoning. He almost didn't make it, but he was stronger and he pulled through. I heard his mother, who would be Adrian Curtis's grandmother, never forgave him for living because the boy who died was her favorite. Doctor told her to have another baby right off. To get over the grief. That baby died two days after it was born. Sometimes I do think this place is cursed like people say, but it's been a blessing for me." She checked her watch. "Gotta get back at it," she said, taking a few steps and giving her apple core a toss into tall grass along a fence. "Good luck."

"Thanks."

Two hours and eight crates of Golden Delicious apples later, it was time for the lunch break. Recalling Georgia's warning, I considered working through it, but my hands were freezing, my legs were tired from standing on cement, and I was hungry. I headed home.

As soon as I stepped in the door, the phone rang and I answered it.

"You don't need to come back this afternoon," Ruth said, her tone distant.

I was surprised, but maybe we'd bagged enough apples for the day. "What time would you like me tomorrow?"

"You don't need to come in tomorrow or the next day. I won't be needing you any longer. Turn in your hours and I'll pay you for this morning."

It took me a few seconds to completely get what she was saying. "Sure." Stunned, I replaced the receiver in the cradle on the kitchen wall. Automatically, I began dragging food from the refrigerator. But as I slapped mayonnaise on a piece of wheat bread, I began to laugh.

A short time later, Adrian appeared, his hair wind raked, his face sunburned. He dropped his jacket over a chair and headed for the kitchen sink, rolling up the sleeves of his flannel shirt.

"Your mother fired me," I said, pressing fingers to my lips to stop my grin.

He turned on the water and reached for the soap. "She did not."

"She did. Swear to God."

"She wouldn't do that." He shut off the water, grabbed a dish towel, and dried his hands. "You must have misunderstood. Did she say you were fired?"

"She didn't use the word *fired*. She didn't have to. She told me she no longer needed me, and I know she's short on help."

"What did you do to make her mad?" He grabbed my sandwich.

"Mayonnaise!" I warned. I squeezed past him to retrieve glasses and plates from the cupboard. "It wasn't me. I thought I was doing a pretty good job. Didn't get as many apples bagged as workers who've been doing it a while, but I kept up."

He took a bite from the sandwich, grimaced, then handed it back. "I'm going to talk to her."

I could see he thought there'd just been some misunderstanding. "Don't do that." She'd probably deny it anyway. There was a reason she'd called me on the phone rather than fire me in the salesroom, where people would overhear.

I quickly set the table, poured two glasses of ice water, opened a bag of Sterzing's potato chips, then sat down with the sandwich finally where it belonged, on my plate. "It doesn't matter. Working in the salesroom was a crazy idea anyway." Ruth wanted me to know I had no place in her world. I shrugged. "Like I said, I'll find a job in Burlington."

He was making his own sandwich now with lunch meat, cheese, pickles, lettuce, and sliced tomato. I could see he still didn't like the idea of my off-site job, so I changed the subject. "I heard some interesting family history while I was over there."

"Oh?" He sat down across from me and added a handful of chips to his plate. I told him a little of what Georgia had shared, leaving out the implication that his mother might have been a gold digger.

"Those sorters are a bunch of gossips," he said. "I can't believe they were telling *you* our family history."

As I recalled Georgia and my deception, I must have gotten a strange look on my face.

"What?" he asked.

"I didn't exactly tell anybody who I was."

I expected anger. Instead, he laughed and said, "Let's go over there right now. I'll introduce you to Georgia. We'll walk in and I'll say, 'I want you to meet my wife.'"

I smiled and shook my head. "There's no way I would do something like that to the poor woman."

"That's what she gets for being such a gossip. Come on." He checked the wall clock. "Before they restart the sorter."

"No!" But I couldn't help laughing along with him. And our combined glee at the idea of pulling such a prank reminded me that he was only a couple of years older than me. A kid. We were both kids. And because I was young, it was easy for me to brush off Ruth's treatment. What difference did it make? It would have been nice if she'd liked me, but I filed the day under adult disapproval, and I could even find her dislike slightly amusing.

CHAPTER TWENTY-EIGHT

I didn't look for a job. I'd planned to, but suddenly I had an idea, something I hadn't thought about in years. I dug out my manual typewriter, bought typing paper, carbon paper, and a new ribbon, and began writing. I kept it a secret for the first week, hiding the typewriter and my accumulating manuscript pages, but one day Adrian dropped by mid-morning, a time that was unusual for him. He caught me sitting at the kitchen table, pawnshop typewriter in front of me. I quickly rolled the paper backward and rested my arm over it.

At the sink, he filled a glass with water, then turned around. "What are you doing?"

"Writing."

"Writing what?"

Oh, he would think it so silly. "A book."

"Book?" The glass in his hand stopped halfway to his mouth. "About what?"

"About a girl who leaves the farm to go to the Amazon."

"Why is she in the Amazon?"

"I don't know. I haven't figured that out yet. But it will have adventure and mystery and romance." My voice rose in excitement.

"What do you know about writing?"

"Nothing." I didn't even know if the pages should be double- or single-spaced. I didn't know how to bind the manuscript once it was finished, or if it was supposed to be bound at all. I had no idea where I would send it once I was done. "But I'll learn. I'll figure it out."

"It seems like a waste of time to me, but if you want to—" *waste your time* were his unspoken words. "I'll bet you type fast. You should be done in a couple of weeks, right?" The book was an intrusion, and I could see he was already looking forward to once again being the center of my world.

"It could take a year." I had to smother a laugh at his shocked expression. To point out that I was committed and he should get used to it, I added, "And when I get the first book done, I'll probably write another."

His bafflement increased. "I don't get why anybody would write one book, let alone two. What will you do with this book if you finish it?"

"Try to sell it to a New York publisher."

"You don't know anyone in New York." A pause. "Do you?"

He might have thought it pure foolishness, but I could also see the wheels turning, and I knew he was thinking about my getting fired by his mother, relieved to know that this little writing project might keep me from driving back and forth to the job I'd talked about finding.

I straightened away from the typewriter, hoping to make it less obvious that I was hiding my work. "You don't think I'll do it, do you? You don't think I'll finish." I had a plan, a goal that was all mine and mine alone.

"It's not that. Stories in books aren't real. I don't know why anybody would want to read one, let alone write one. I don't know why you're doing it. People read fiction to escape. Are you writing to escape? To create something you don't have here?"

"I just want to tell a story. I don't know if I'll be able to sell it, but I'll write it."

He finished his water, put down the glass, and came to stand behind me, rubbing my shoulders as we talked. "What about drawing?"

"I'll still draw, but I'm never going to be very good."

"You will. You are."

I shook my head. "I don't think so." Doubts about my artistic talent had increased, maybe because of my exposure to Adrian. He was a real artist. Drawing came naturally to him. He loved it.

It occurred to me that I owed my new endeavor to Ruth, and I could already imagine the dedication page: *To my mother-in-law. Thanks for firing me.*

If she'd embraced me, if she'd welcomed me, if she hadn't fired me, I might not have been so driven. I might not have pulled out my type-writer or ever thought about writing a book. And maybe Adrian's impli-cations had some truth to them. Maybe my writing had less to do with the need to create and more to do with the need to carve out something for myself, give myself a sense of purpose. Something that reached beyond the farm, beyond the apples that were to be arranged just so, five on the bottom so the plastic bag wouldn't tip over. And I told myself that I didn't need to be a part of their world of apples, no matter how sweet the smell.

As the days and weeks passed, I worked steadily. I tried not to flaunt my new career path. I never left typed pages lying around. And if I stopped in the middle of a page, I rolled the paper so the text wasn't visible. But sometimes I would forget, or Adrian would stop by unexpectedly, and I'd catch him reading a stray paragraph or a description. And he would look hurt and betrayed, like a jealous husband who'd come across a strange phone number in his wife's purse.

CHAPTER TWENTY-NINE

"Could you be pregnant?" the doctor asked in a heavy German accent.

I sat on the edge of the exam table, wrapped in thin crinkly paper. "No...I mean, well..." My stomach took a dive.

Pregnant?

The period following my grandmother's death had been a strange combination of time moving quickly and time moving slowly. Yes, I'd been feeling sick and weak and sleepy, but I thought it was depression.

"I'll have the nurse draw some blood so we can rule out a few things," the doctor said. "We'll run a pregnancy test at the same time."

The nurse tapped a vein and filled three small vials. "Go ahead and get dressed. I'll be back in a few minutes with your iron level."

I was anemic. Vitamins and iron were prescribed. But I wasn't off the hook. "Call back in three days for the pregnancy results," the nurse said.

I returned to the farm, but I didn't say anything to Adrian other than to tell him about the anemia. Surely I wasn't pregnant. Impossible.

I thought of the girls in the car, the wedding-shower girls and their talk of babies. How foreign it had seemed, how remote and as far from me as a life could possibly be. I didn't know what worried me more. The idea of having an infant to care for or the idea of being a mother.

Three days later I drove to Burlington to call the doctor's office. I went the twelve miles because I wanted to be alone when I made the call. I didn't want Adrian walking in on me while I was on the phone, and I took comfort in putting the span of the Mississippi River between the farm and me. The Mississippi had always worked as a dividing line between two places, no matter what side of the river I was on.

I pulled into the Montgomery Ward parking lot to use the drive-up pay phone, which sat along the heavily traveled Mount Pleasant Avenue. Immediately after I dialed, traffic noise picked up.

The receptionist answered. I shouted my name and told her I was calling to get my test results.

She was gone a moment, then returned with a clatter of heavy plastic. A pause, then a response I couldn't quite decipher.

"Positive?" Had I heard right? "Positive?" I repeated. "What does that mean?"

A semi trailer accelerated in front of me. I breathed diesel fumes.

"You're pregnant."

"Pregnant?" I was still shouting, but I had to make absolutely sure I had the correct information.

"Yes."

I put the receiver back and rolled up the window.

Someone honked, and I looked in the rearview mirror to see an angry face in the car behind me. I pulled forward a couple of vehicle lengths. Then I did what I always did in moments of high stress—I reached for my cigarettes. I lit up and took a deep drag.

And immediately realized I shouldn't be smoking.

I took another drag. And another.

Okay, calm down.

It's not like a baby was going to pop out of me at any second. Nine months. But how far along was I? A month? Maybe two? God, I had no idea. I knew nothing about babies. I didn't even know anybody who *had* a baby.

I couldn't handle being married. How could I have a baby?

Back home, I told Adrian about the pregnancy. He turned white, got up from the kitchen table, and left the house. I would have done the same thing. But to his credit, he returned an hour later.

"I'm sorry," he said. "It just took me by surprise. I've always wanted kids. I've always wanted to be a father."

But his mother didn't take the news as well.

"Don't tell anybody," she said as soon as she heard. She'd made a special trip to our house and now sat in the living room at one end of the green couch.

"Why?" I could understand if she was worried that people might think the pregnancy came before the wedding, but that wasn't the case. It wouldn't have bothered me, but it would have meant public humiliation for her.

"You might have a miscarriage, so it's pointless to tell people so early in the pregnancy."

"A miscarriage? What are you talking about?"

"You might not have a baby." She fixed me with a hard stare, as if trying to transmit something she couldn't say aloud. "Don't tell a soul. Once one person knows, the whole county will know."

"So?" Her odd behavior and odder directive both frightened me and irritated me. *Just say what you mean.*

"One day you might be pregnant, and the next you might not be pregnant anymore."

Her words certainly held a sinister quality, and I couldn't help but imagine her pushing me down a flight of stairs or some such nonsense, but I soon realized she was implying that pregnancies often ended in miscarriages, at least on the farm.

I'd never given my health much thought, and for the past year or so I'd lived on a diet of alcohol, beef sticks, pickled eggs, and Stewart's sandwiches. But shortly after I found out I was pregnant, maternal instinct kicked in. I quit drinking and smoking, and I began eating nutritious meals. I didn't experience any threat of miscarriage, and the pregnancy moved along uneventfully except for a strange, recurring dream in which I was pregnant with a calf. After giving birth in the dream, I carried the slimy animal around in wet newspapers. "Here's my baby! Look at my baby!" I would show it to people, and they would recoil. "What's wrong?" I'd ask. "Haven't you ever seen a cow baby? A human cow baby?"

CHAPTER THIRTY

"I was thinking maybe we should start looking for our own place soon," I said.

Harvest was over, the cider press was running, the air smelled like apples, and Adrian and I were sitting at our tiny kitchen table.

"You mean a place to live?" Adrian asked. "We have a place. This place."

My pregnancy had quickly taken us from newlyweds who knew nothing about each other to stodgy married couple who knew nothing about each other. "We can't stay here forever, especially with a baby coming."

"This is where the hired man lives, and that's what I am. The hired man."

"You're the son." I was surprised to find that a place so embedded in history and past generations was run like a cold, impersonal business. "You mean you've never had any plans to move at least into your own house? I'm not talking about moving away." We'd already had that conversation.

"Where would I move? *Why* would I move?"

"I don't know where. Up the road."

"My parents would never allow it."

"That's ridiculous." This new issue hadn't even been on my radar. "What about the East Place?" The farmhouse had a private lane and a huge yard. It was less than a mile from the main house but out of eye-sight.

"A renter is living there."

Practically for free. In return he kept an eye on things and paid for repairs. We could do that. "Can't he be given notice? Maybe we could move in the spring? Or in a year?" Just knowing it would eventually happen would make the present situation more tolerable.

He shook his head. "You don't get it. This is where I'm supposed to live."

"What difference does it make as long as you show up when you're supposed to? And if this house were empty, there would be more places for the pickers to stay. I'd think your parents would like that."

"Come with me to talk to them. You'll see what I'm up against."

We crossed the yard to the big house and entered through the front office, a room that jutted from the original building. From the desk, a person had a clear view of the driveway and the salesroom.

The farmhouse still contained a vague hint of the past. You knew the bones of the structure existed beneath the green shag carpet and the Grecian mural. In the kitchen, sayings covered the walls and refrigerator. Things like "A Big Wife and a Big Barn Never Did a Man Any Harm." And "Ewes Not Fat, Ewes Fluffy."

Adrian's parents sat facing each other at the kitchen table, a package of caramel rolls between them, his father in denim overalls and a red seed-corn cap, his mother in her signature gingham shirt and dark jeans. Pans of uneaten food had grown cold on the stove, and the kitchen smelled of strong coffee. Adrian poured himself a cup and sat down in the chair that was still his chair. I took the remaining seat.

There was some discussion about the plans for the rest of the day, and what apples were getting low in the salesroom, and what apples needed to be replenished from the underground storage area; then Adrian cleared his throat and broached the subject of our moving.

His parents looked at each other, and I could instantly see that Adrian hadn't exaggerated their feelings about the subject. Adrian's father made eye contact with me, and I almost recoiled at the iciness I saw there. Then he turned to his son. "If you move, don't bother ever coming around here again. You won't be welcome."

Ruth made a strange choking noise, kind of a cross between a sob and a sound meant to soothe.

The older man got to his feet, chair scraping. "I'm going back out to the cider room."

That was that. Final word.

He left all three of us sitting there. Ruth started clearing the table. "You know how he feels about that kind of thing."

Adrian shrugged and looked at me. *See what I mean?* He wasn't upset. No, he seemed a little relieved. What if his dad had said he was okay with the idea? Would Adrian have left?

I was back to the puzzle of why Adrian had married me. By his own admission, he didn't know. But my life had been everything his wasn't. No family ties, no responsibility, no guilt, no heritage, no land that went back generations. Maybe that was it. Maybe I represented a life he could never have even if he wanted it. But I'd brought none of my world with me, and I couldn't shake the notion that he'd left the farm, found a curiosity, and brought me home, the very deviation of our actions setting in motion a series of unforeseen and out-of-synch anomalies. My recent life had been uneventful before Adrian showed up. My grandmother had been healthy. We'd put up strawberry jam a few short months ago. And then there was the car wreck, and not one but two dead horses.

The Curtis curse.

I tried to tell myself I didn't believe in such nonsense, but at the same time I feared my denial might bring more bad luck. But to embrace it. . . That was asking for trouble.

"That house is for you," Ruth told her son. "Why would you want to live anywhere else?" She gave me a hard look. "This is your fault. You're too independent."

"That's a bad thing?" I suddenly understood that Adrian's parents saw me as a threat to their way of life. Absurd. What kind of threat could someone like me be? What impact could someone like me possibly have on the future of the farm?

"Of course independence is bad," she said, implying that anyone who thought otherwise was an idiot.

Adrian got to his feet. "Let's go."

We walked home in silence, and I sat down on the front stoop.

"I thought my dad would be more sympathetic." Adrian lit a cigarette and I inhaled the aroma. "He didn't want to stay here when he and my mother were married. He wanted a place of his own. I think my grandparents would have been okay with it as long as they didn't live too far away, but my mother talked my dad into staying."

I put out my hand, and he passed me the cigarette. I'd quit buying and smoking my own, but I couldn't resist the occasional drag from his. One puff or two about did it because the filterless Camels were harsh. I'd quit for good in another week or so. "You're okay with living here?" I asked. "Honestly?"

"It's free. If we moved, we'd have house payments. This place is a big part of my income."

I'd been around long enough to know how much money he made. Barely enough for a single person to scrape by, let alone a family. "You're basically their slave. Practically free labor." I used to bemoan my lack of parental guidance and involvement, but Adrian's tangled relationship with his parents and the farm was something I was just beginning to grasp and would most likely never understand.

"The farm will be mine one day." He shrugged. "But right now I'm just a worker bee."

"When will it be yours? In forty years?" I knew I sounded exactly like the outsider I was. Someone intruding on their utopia, full of ideas that would only cause friction in what was a smoothly running system. But the archaic hierarchy, along with Adrian's acceptance of it, astounded me.

I wasn't sure it was worth staying, but then I didn't understand having such a strong connection to a specific parcel of land, a connection that went back generations. Even if he moved, he'd have to live with the guilt of abandoning the farm and his parents.

For me, it was unfathomable to have your whole life mapped out before you were born. And here I was, soon to give birth to the next generation.

CHAPTER THIRTY-ONE

The first Christmas was spent at the big farmhouse. Sunlight falling in the giant windows was unforgiving and unrelenting, illuminating the Grecian décor and the shag carpet. A football game blared on the television, and everybody including Adrian's unmarried brother and sister gave off an aura of wishing they were somewhere else.

Conversation was dull, and the food was bland—a lot of pastel side dishes made with Jell-O, colored marshmallows, and Cool Whip. I found myself wondering if this was how normal people lived. This shared tedium put under a magnifying glass a few times a year. I couldn't fully grasp why it was so awful. Maybe because it was just a group of people doing what was expected of them, with no surprises and no joy. The holidays of my life may have been volatile, but they'd come with good food and wine, music, introspective discussions, and laughter.

None of Adrian's family seemed to really know one another. They occupied the same space but seemed shut off, closed off, secretive, and repressed. The conversation was the conversation of strangers, with awkwardly introduced topics that fizzled out until someone came up with something else just as impossible.

Did they ever raise their voices? Did they ever shout? Or get excited?

Did they ever talk about anything deep or personal? Did they ever share their feelings and emotions?

Even though Adrian's brother and sister no longer lived on the farm, it was easy to see they were still defined by it. And always would be. *This is who I am. This is where I'm from.* Without the farm, would they exist? Or would they turn into bits of dried-up dust? I got the sense that they were all being held together from the outside. They were who they were because of the farm, because its soil and the generations buried in it bound them to life.

Conversation shifted to farming and a topic I didn't understand about purchasing chemicals with a special applicator's license. Once Adrian and I left the farmhouse, I brought up the discussion.

"Why was your dad so intent on buying so many drums of pesticide?" I asked as we walked back to our little house. The temperature was below zero, and the snow had a crust that would hold for a moment, then break.

"The EPA is always banning important chemicals, and we have to stock up while they're still available," Adrian said. "We all have a license so we can purchase several seasons' worth."

I looked at him in shock.

"Everybody does it," he said. "*Everybody.* We couldn't survive otherwise. Do you know how hard it is to kill the codling moth? They can wipe out an orchard. Especially the old orchard because those trees aren't as disease resistant. Once they bore into the trunk and lay their eggs, that's it. It's too late. Farmers know what works in their fields, and they know what doesn't. And there's a misconception that new products are safer. It's all bad. It's all dangerous. The new stuff just hasn't been banned yet."

I didn't like what I was hearing. I thought about the fields that began outside our door and stretched to the horizon.

"The Midwest has a higher concentration of insects than the East or West Coast," Adrian said. "And decades of pesticide use have created resistance. It's going to take stronger and stronger chemicals for farmers to stay in business, not weaker ones."

Inside, we hung our coats and stocking caps by the back door and kicked off our boots. My cheeks felt cold and smooth to the touch. "They should stop," I said.

He laughed at my unrealistic comment.

"No, really. Go organic."

"It can't be done. Maybe somebody with a few acres could go organic as a hobby or side project, but it's too labor-intensive for a full-size farm. Plus, the codling moth would take over. And most importantly, everybody would think we were nuts, and they'd be right."

"You can't be concerned about that."

He tossed his gray wool scarf over a chair, and I wondered if he felt the relief I felt at being back in our own space. Probably not. "It's too late," he said. "We've already gone too far. Farms are too big, and chemicals have created superbugs and superweeds. It's too late to turn around. The EPA might be looking out for the average person, but nobody is looking out for the farmer. It's us against them."

"Do you really believe that?" If anything, the EPA probably wasn't being strict enough. And what about children? How dangerous was it to have a child in the middle of such toxic saturation?

But people had kids around here all the time, I reassured myself. Adrian had grown up here. He was healthy. His father had worked around chemicals most of his life. Really bad things like DDT, and he was okay. He wasn't sick. And how could you blame farmers for choosing to believe that they weren't poisoning the world and their own children?

CHAPTER THIRTY-TWO

Albuquerque, New Mexico, 1969

At age fourteen, I ran away from home.

I'd been sent from Artesia to Albuquerque, New Mexico, to stay a week with people I didn't know so my mother and David could play honeymoon. I understood their desire to be alone. It had to be tough for newlyweds to have a teenager sleeping in a room a few feet away. The perfect solution was to send me to a town I missed—Albuquerque. The strangers I visited had a daughter my age, a beautiful girl with flawless skin, large gray eyes, and straight blond hair that hung past her waist, a girl who came handpicked by my mother—someone with a solid track record for latching onto the biggest loser in the room.

The girl, whose name was Jodie, turned out to be a soulless bitch who filled her home with drugs and equally soulless, sex-crazed boys while her parents were at work, and who talked about slicing her parents' throats while they slept. Jodie would have done Charles Manson proud.

After marijuana was discovered in Jodie's room, my mother arrived in Albuquerque to tell us that Jodie and I were being sent to a "home." Being shipped off didn't sound that bad, but I was pretty sure a "home" involved getting locked up with a lot of girls like the psycho bitch who'd gotten me into this mess. I imagined masculine women with tight perms, beige walking shoes, and floral housedresses, making me get down on my hands and knees to scrub stone floors. Later, I would beg for gruel: "More, please."

While everyone slept, Jodie and I ran off, parting ways once we hit the city streets.

As the days passed without food or sleep, my judgment—what little I had—vanished, and somehow I ended up in a house full of junkies. To get to their place, I took a fire escape up the side of a weed- and trash-littered cement-block building, then crossed a pea-gravel roof where sunlight steamed beer urine and rotting fast food, to a door that opened to a room littered with mattresses.

Right away I could tell the serious professionals from the frauds. The professional junkies had slack jaws, thin arms, and desolate eyes. Then there were the shiny suburban kids who were visiting for a thrill—or maybe they'd arrived by accident. Heard about a party, or a place where somebody was old enough to buy beer. Maybe there would even be sex. They'd stepped inside and—whoa. Junkies everywhere.

I was young and confused, so it was no surprise that a guy talked me into letting him dilute some heroin with water so he could shoot me up and turn me on. Before he pulled the rubber tourniquet from my arm I felt the magic wash through me and fell back on a mattress.

Heroin junkies might look dead on the outside, but inside it's heaven. Inside it's the absence of everything bad. It's beautiful and perfect, and when you're inside, the last thing you think about is dying because you want that perfect moment to last forever.

But perfection is an illusion. Perfection has a price.

During those perfect moments while I was tethered to the bed by drugs, bad things happened to me. Very bad things that I will never talk about.

Once I was able to function, I left the junkie house. Two blocks away, someone stopped me.

"Hey, you in trouble? You need some help?" He was young. Hispanic. He told me his name was Manuel, and his eyes were soft and concerned.

"You need a place to stay? I know a place. A nice place. I can take you there."

The kind tone of his voice hooked me.

I hopped on the back of his motorcycle, rode across town to the desert, where more bad things happened.

There was no nice place to stay, and Manuel told me he'd been at the junkie house. He said he'd followed me outside. At least he didn't leave me in the middle of the desert. He gave me a ride back to town, and the weird thing is that I found myself feeling grateful that he hadn't left me out there and that he hadn't tortured me with the knife he'd held to my throat.

The lesson I learned was that some people will take what they want, whenever they want, with no guilt or thought of the consequences, and that evil people existed to prey upon the innocent. But from experience, I also knew cruelty wasn't always delivered by strangers. Sometimes abuse came directly from the people who should have cared the most, and it could take place in the dark heart of any family.

I couldn't go back into the junkie house. Once Manuel dropped me off, I walked to a grim neighborhood drugstore, swiped a pack of razor blades, and found a nice quiet spot under a cement overpass.

Fourteen and I was tired of living.

I'd heard that bleeding to death was painless. I'd heard it was peaceful and you just drifted off.

An absence of fear.

And wasn't that what we all wanted?

For the fear to stop? Isn't that really what it was all about? The drugs? The running away?

I thought about the plate of poison mushrooms, about how I should have died years ago. With the razor blade, I made a test slice. Even though it wasn't deep, a red line formed on the pale skin of my inner wrist. I found myself mesmerized by the white and red.

There was more than one way to escape what had happened to me.

I tossed the blade away, and in that moment I made up my mind. I would never tell anybody about the heroin and the junkie house and the bad things that had happened there. I wouldn't tell anybody about my motorcycle ride to the desert.

There are things you don't talk about. There are things you don't want people to know because as soon as they know, you change. You become someone different in their eyes.

I wasn't sent to a home, and when my mother asked where I'd been all those days, I lied. I told her I'd hidden in a storage shed.

As far as you're concerned.

If she knew my secret, it would give her power over me; I would become weaker in her eyes. I couldn't allow that. Maybe these were just excuses. Maybe if nobody else knew, then I could erase the night. I could pretend it had never happened.

"Don't tell anyone about running away," my mother instructed. "David has a reputation to uphold in this town. If anyone asks about your weight loss, say you got food poisoning."

As far as you're concerned.

CHAPTER THIRTY-THREE

Winter turned to spring, and I gradually began to accept farming risks as a part of life. Like coal miners who know their job is dangerous, or artists who work with lead and bronze. Every occupation can impact a person's health. These were the excuses I made, and the fact that nobody was dropping dead lulled me into a false sense of security.

As the land awakened around me, I saw the farm as something to cherish, as something beautiful and timeless and unique. Even from my close vantage point, it sometimes seemed only a little short of paradise.

When summer came, I photographed round hay bales resting against the light and shadow of softly rolling hills. Giant orange suns setting over hazy cornfields and behind windmills. Beautiful red barns and cabins abandoned in dark woods.

I captured the pattern of the mowed fields, but I could never capture a green so deep it hurt, or the secret organic scent of the ground when it's been sliced open with a plow blade. That couldn't be captured with a camera lens or a pen. That sweet ache of nature and time that kept invisibly moving, no matter how much you wanted it to stop.

*   *   *

A year after I started my new life with Adrian, we had a baby boy we named Alexander.

The birth of a grandson brought about a change in my relationship with Ruth. I was suddenly tolerated because I'd supplied the farm with an heir. When I knocked at the back door, Ruth invited me inside, but I was always treated like an odd guest she really didn't want around, ignored unless we were discussing the baby.

The farm and the ground and Alexander's heritage must have reached him in utero, because the first word he spoke was *apple*. I initially thought it an odd coincidence—I'd simply applied the obvious to his baby sounds. But no. While the two syllables weren't exactly correct, they were close enough, and tests with images and actual apples brought the same results, almost as if he'd arrived with an awareness of his destiny.

"Ap-pah."

Ruth beamed, and bounced my baby on her knee. "Bless his heart. He already knows he's going to be an apple farmer." In that moment she claimed him for her own and for the farm.

As further evidence of Alexander's defection, his favorite toy was his grandmother's gift of a Happy Apple—a big plastic apple with an obnoxious smiling face. The toy rocked and chimed, and Alexander latched onto it the way other children latch onto stuffed animals and blankets. He lay in his crib and cooed, he and the apple having their own private conversation. Once he was strong enough, he lifted the apple by the stem and dropped it from his high chair to my bare toes. While I hobbled in pain, he laughed in delight and slapped the tray with both palms.

I wrote while Alexander napped, and when the manuscript was finished I put it in a typing-paper box and mailed it to addresses I found printed in the front of books. Months later, the manuscript would return with a rejection letter, and I would rework the material and send it out again.

Three years after typing that first page, I received an offer from a major publishing house. The editor called my story a character study.

Artists seek validation and approval, and maybe I was seeking it more than most. Unlike Adrian, I would never have been satisfied to leave the manuscript in a drawer. It wasn't enough to have written it; my words had to be read.

There was no celebration of my sale, no wine or champagne or dinner. Adrian was skeptical of the contract, and even when a box of paperbacks arrived, he was unimpressed. Adrian was an artist, yet he could never fully embrace art. Art for him was a secret thing, a shameful thing, done in privacy.

I quietly put the advance money in the bank, because there was nothing we wanted, nothing we needed. We had it already. A nearly perfect life on a beautiful farm.

CHAPTER THIRTY-FOUR

Sometimes there are people you must forget because of the damage they cause—blood ties or not. My mother was one of those people. I could have attached psychological and psychiatric labels to her, but I wouldn't.

Months would pass with only a select few knowing her whereabouts. At unexpected moments, a gift I'd given her as a child would show up in the mailbox. No return address, always postmarked from a new area of the country, accompanied by a cruel letter, or by nothing at all.

"From her?" Adrian would ask if he saw me holding the unopened package, my face blank.

We rarely talked about my family or my past. It was almost as if I'd sprung full-grown from the ground, a person with no history, no ties, no complications. But he found amusement in my mother's random mailbox intrusions into our life, possibly because the occasional proof of my dysfunctional family made his own seem less abnormal. Always a good thing.

As much as I could deny that the packages hit their intended target, it wasn't entirely true.

Being a single mother must have been hard, and it must have been especially hard to have your life derailed by children you resented.

If my brothers and I had been dogs, she would have dumped us on a back road far from town in the hopes that we would never find our way home. But she'd been stuck with us, and I almost felt sorry for her.

I kept in touch with my brothers, usually one or two phone calls a year, those conversations tempered with caution and oddly mixed with pain, as if we knew too much about one another's past, but not enough about the present. The common ground we shared was our mother, and we compared notes on who'd heard from her last, what the package had contained, did it come with a twenty-five-page letter that revised our history, but never failed to blame us for ruining her life? Was the letter read or thrown away? Was a return address included? The answer to this last was almost always no.

From old acquaintances, we heard odd snippets, stories of who she was fighting with, or the most recent pet she'd had David shoot when it failed to live up to expectations.

"Open it," Adrian coaxed as we stood in the road near the mailbox.

"No."

"Then let me."

"No." I refused to be his entertainment.

Later, after he'd returned to the field and I was alone in the kitchen, I opened the manila envelope. Inside was a piece of artwork I'd given my mother for Christmas, back when the Pilot House was a real house, back when we'd celebrated holidays there.

It was a photo of an apple cut from a magazine. A shiny Red Delicious.

The past came rushing back, and I remembered lying on my mother's bed while I pasted the image to a piece of green construction paper, fascinated and mesmerized by the beauty of the apple. I could almost smell the crayons, almost feel how hard I'd pressed against the paper.

To fashion a frame, I'd used the lid from a box of silk stockings. The crude craft was supposed to be a Christmas card, and at the time I'd worried that the choice of an apple would annoy her, because what did an apple have to do with Christmas?

The arrival of the childhood artwork made me wonder if my life was as preordained as Adrian's, just in a less obvious way. A photo from a magazine. An apple.

CHAPTER THIRTY-FIVE

Three years after our son was born, we had another child. A daughter we named Lucia. Being female and not the firstborn, Lucia didn't arrive with a designated role; she didn't arrive with a script. She could be whatever and whoever she wanted to be. Her first word was *Momma*, her second *Dada*. And it was a long time before she could say the word *apple*.

Adrian and I embraced parenthood and our own little family unit, and we both discovered that children were very easy to love. The four of us were inseparable. From the time they were infants, Alexander and Lucia spent every moment with us whether we were inside or out, the hours filled with silly talk, laughter, and private jokes we shared with no one else.

Ruth rarely ventured past her yard. She never visited the fields or timber, so the entire farm felt like our private world. The pond behind our house especially felt like our place. I would pack a picnic basket, and we would spend afternoons fishing and evenings sitting in front of a bonfire. We started Alexander and Lucia on ice skates before they were three years old, and winter evenings were spent skating and playing pond hockey.

In the summer, we planted, mowed, baled, and put up hay with the children beside us. We fed cattle together; we ate lunch and dinner together. After dinner there were more chores to be done. Sometimes I remained behind to write, and when the three of them returned, the door would open on a burst of laughter.

"Will you draw with me?" a six-year-old Lucia asked later in the evening. And she and Adrian would lie on the floor and draw on separate sketch pads, Adrian offering advice while I typed away in the corner and Alexander pored through my record album collection.

Alexander was infatuated with sixties and seventies music. He spent hours studying album artwork and asking about bands and wanting to know what the world had been like when good music and entire albums were played on regular radio stations. In the truck, he turned the dial to KFMH 99 Plus, a format-free station broadcasting out of Muscatine, Iowa. Drawing frustrated him, and music gave him a foothold in the creative world.

Every evening, I read Alexander and Lucia a bedtime story in their shared room, kissed them, and turned out the light.

"Good night! Sleep tight!" Lucia would call sweetly, smacking her lips against her palm.

"Adios! Adios, amiga!" Alexander finished.

As our children grew, the Sweet Melinda trees grew with them. The trunks became thick and sturdy, the branches strong enough to tolerate high winds without breaking. The bark was smooth and shiny, with small ridges characteristic of apple trees.

Each spring a few random blossoms appeared, but the buds refused to set, while all around them other varieties thrived. Each season marked another year of waiting for yet another spring and new blossoms. I began to fear that Adrian's trees weren't hardy enough for our winters. Maybe the blossoms would never set. Maybe the trees would never produce a single apple.

For Adrian, the Sweet Melindas were his and his alone, and I wanted him to succeed, not because of the apples, but because of what they represented. They were a chance for him to establish his place on the farm, a chance to prove he was more than just hard labor and a worker bee. They would prove his worth in a place where worth shouldn't have to be proven.

CHAPTER THIRTY-SIX

My grandmother always said the best time to find morel mushrooms was when lilacs weren't yet blooming and oak leaves were the size of squirrels' ears. Every old-timer had a different theory of how and where to find the spongy morsels, but everyone agreed on one thing: morels took a good rain, quickly followed by warmth and sunshine, to make them pop through the soil.

It was early spring, and our little family of four left the house on foot, plastic bags tucked into the back pockets of our jeans, to hike through timber that bordered the orchard and surrounded pastures and cornfields.

On this particular Sunday afternoon, the ground was soft from the previous night's rain, the sky was a brilliant blue, and the temperature was in the midseventies. Perfect mushrooming weather. The little gray morels came early, when the days were cold and the nights colder, but the sun now fell warm upon dark ground, coaxing the yellow morels out of hiding. We just had to find them.

Unlike the skeleton canopy above our heads, the timber floor had already awakened. Near narrow, twisting streams, moss covered rocks in a carpet of lush green, and jack-in-the-pulpits hid beneath mayapples. After a deep winter, the air smelled of last fall's leaves, decaying trees, and awakening, spring growth. In two months, the path we were on would be too dense for hiking.

At some point in the past, nature had tumbled giant trees to the ground, accidentally and conveniently creating bridges that spanned small ravines. We tested the fallen trees, and then crossed, sometimes walking, sometimes straddling the trunk and scooting to the other side. I don't know if the afternoon was really about the mushrooms, or more about a visit to a secret world, a place that would soon be impassible, swallowed by vegetation.

After two hours, our plastic bags still empty, we broke out of the winter-chilled timber into a warm field of rolling pasture. In the distance, Adrian's horse, Mr. Red, spotted us and whinnied. Hooves beat on soft ground, clumps of mud and grass flying behind him as he raced across the open pasture to greet us, pulling to an abrupt halt just feet away. He still wore his shaggy winter coat, and he looked like a giant teddy bear. It no longer seemed strange that Mr. Red wasn't kept in a barn and was allowed to roam the pastures and timber at will. Adrian checked on him daily, feeding him oats and corn in cold weather, making sure he had access to shelter if needed. Mr. Red seemed a myth, a part of nature itself.

Adrian made a stirrup with locked fingers and hefted ten-year-old Alexander onto the horse's back. "Grab his mane," Adrian instructed. "There you go." Then he lifted Lucia up behind her brother. "Hang on," he told her.

Even though she'd only just turned seven, she was independent, and I could tell she'd rather be on the horse by herself.

"Don't kick him," Adrian warned.

"Will he run?" she asked.

"You better believe it," her father said.

"How old is Mr. Red?" Alexander wanted to know. Our son had dark hair and dark eyes, looking more like me, but acting more like Adrian—introspective, with a clever sense of humor.

"I got him when I was in high school," Adrian said, "so he's probably around fifteen."

"How long will he live?" Alexander already understood that death was a part of farm life.

"Fifteen is getting up there," his father told him. "Horses don't live as long as people."

"I don't want Mr. Red to die!" Lucia wailed.

"Some horses live thirty years." Adrian didn't add that those horses were probably in *The Guinness Book of Records*.

"What animals live a long time?" Lucia asked.

"Elephants," I told her. "Should we get an elephant?"

"Yes!" both kids chimed.

With Adrian on one side of the horse and me on the other, we strolled through the pasture, pausing on a knoll that marked the highest point of the farm. In the distance, the bluff ended and the bottoms began. Ten miles across that flat, treeless expanse was the Mississippi River, and before the river, my uncle's bar. I'd been thinking of him a lot lately, and right then and there I decided I would visit him soon, regardless of the reception.

Mr. Red stopped with us, hung his head, and closed his eyes, the weight on his back and the sun making him drowsy. Adrian and I helped the kids down, and once they had both feet on the ground I stuck my nose in the horse's coat and inhaled. "I love the way he smells."

Adrian laughed and shook his head.

If I'd been a betting person, I wouldn't have expected our marriage to last. We were too different. But in some ways we were very much alike, and I think we'd grown more alike over time. I could look at Adrian's face and easily read his thoughts, and we often said the same thing at the same time. We shared a respect for nature, art, and creativity, we both wanted a peaceful home life, and we had two sweet children.

I still wasn't sure what married love was all about, and I wasn't sure I'd recognize it if I saw it. Just saying you loved someone didn't make it so. But I thought maybe Adrian loved me. And I thought maybe I loved him. I wondered if this day was what love felt like. Not about words, but about time and peace and contentment. About trust and children, about reading expressions and finishing each other's sentences.

Adrian sprawled out on the ground, and Lucia and Alexander tumbled on top of him. Adrian winked and reached out his hand for me. I grasped it and lay down beside him while the children held a serious and silly conversation that had nothing to do with adults. Sleepy, I rolled to my back, closed my eyes, and became aware of bees, birds, and Mr. Red's blunt teeth rubbing together as he bit, ripped, and chewed grass. A few minutes later, Lucia woke me up, tickling my neck with clover, her blue eyes just inches from my face.

"We haven't found any mushrooms!" she said. Now that I was awake, she launched an attack on her dad.

He braced his hands under her armpits and lifted her in the air above him, her long, blond curls bouncing. "You don't even like mushrooms," he said.

"I like to find them."

Lucia was bold and fearless, eager to embrace the unknown, a little alien in our midst.

"Will you eat any?" Adrian asked.

"No."

"I won't either!" Alexander said, raking his fingers through the horse's mane.

"What about you?" Adrian asked me.

"I had kind of a bad experience with mushrooms."

The ground was getting damp, and the sun was going down. We got to our feet, preparing to head home.

"I want to show you something," Adrian said.

Anxious to hang on to the day as long as they could, the children followed their father to the flat stone he and I had visited that afternoon before we'd ever talked about marriage. Because it was early spring, the stone was easy to find, but I knew from summers past that it would soon be hidden by deep grass.

"It's a grave," Adrian told them. "A teenage girl is buried here. She was a pioneer, probably on her way to St. Louis with her family."

I picked a handful of tiny yellow flowers and placed them in the center of the stone. "She died of something called diphtheria," I said, finishing the legend but leaving out the more disturbing aspects. One day the story would be passed to the next generation. Alexander and Lucia would have children. Adrian and I would take them mushroom hunting, and we would bring them here and show them the grave and tell them the story.

"It's such a sad spot," I said. As soon as I said it, I wondered at my words, because it wasn't sad at all. It was beautiful, but an odd sensation had washed over me—an unfounded fear of something I couldn't yet see.

"Sad? This is exactly the kind of place I'd like to be buried," Adrian said. "Close to nature, not in some flat, treeless cemetery."

Alexander and Lucia put their hands on the rock, feeling its warmth, thinking about a mysterious girl who'd lived long ago. Adrian and I smiled at each other across the dark and light heads of our children.

CHAPTER THIRTY-SEVEN

The next morning I baked an apple pie and drove to my uncle's. The bar wasn't open, so I walked around back and knocked on the trailer door. Uncle Jim answered and stared at me a second, his expression shifting from cautious to pleased.

Standing at the bottom of the steps, I lifted the pie pan covered with clear wrap. "It's still warm."

Inside, we sat at the kitchen table and ate pie on paper plates while listening to Paul Harvey. The trailer smelled like a septic tank, dust, stale laundry, and whatever was cooking in the Crock-Pot.

"I never thought your marriage would last," my uncle said. "Mainly because of the mother." His hair had turned gray, but his eyes were as intense as ever.

"You were right about her," I said. "And right about my having no clue about what I was getting into."

"This is good." He pointed his white plastic fork at his slice of pie.

Crumble topping flavored with cinnamon and nutmeg, sprinkled over a combination of Jonathan and Winesap apples, plus a few Golden Delicious for natural sweetness. I'd done a lot of experimenting over the years, and I'd learned how to bake an amazing apple pie. I didn't use measurements, so every pie was different, every pie a surprise.

"I know how one bad choice can change a person's life forever," he said.

"You're talking about what happened in Chicago. The murder." He'd never discussed it with me, and I had the feeling he'd never discussed it with anybody.

He nodded. Then, surprisingly, he elaborated. "My car was packed, and I was leaving for your place in Albuquerque. The guy who'd committed the murder showed up at the last minute, said he wasn't doing anything and wanted to help drive. Get out of the city for a few days. As simple as that."

They came for the visit, but I hardly remembered his friend. Young, quiet, just kind of there. They stayed a couple of days before heading back. At some point on the return trip, Uncle Jim's photo hit the front page of the *Chicago Tribune*. Both men were arrested, my uncle immediately fired.

I wasn't sure what kind of job Uncle Jim had in Chicago, but at one time he'd been part of a team that had designed spacecrafts for early *Apollo* missions. I'd seen photos of him standing next to a command module, the kind that dropped into the ocean.

He deserved better than paper plates and plastic forks and a trailer that smelled like a sewer.

"Have you ever thought about selling the bar?" I asked, then immediately regretted my question. Who was I to come up with rash solutions to problems that couldn't be solved and would only make things worse. He'd grown used to this life, and sometimes the familiar was better than the promise of something better.

"What would I do?" he asked.

"Travel?"

"I don't need to go anywhere. And the customers—they're my family."

I nodded, understanding, and we both took another bite of pie.

"I've been reading about you in the paper," he said. "About your writing career. Books on the bestseller list. Awards. A lot of people dream about becoming a writer, and you just quietly did it."

"I won't accept defeat—that's all. That's the biggest secret to making it in the writing world. Being stubborn."

"But the talent has to be there."

I smiled. One rule I'd taken away from Catholic school was never to brag or talk about myself. "Maybe."

Later, I used the bathroom and saw that the moss was still in the toilet. I was glad to see it.

CHAPTER THIRTY-EIGHT

Artesia, New Mexico, 1972

Three years after we moved to Artesia, the college where David taught lost its accreditation and folded, and my mother and stepfather and younger brother left for a new adventure while I stuck around in order to graduate. Once I had my high school diploma, I moved into a little rental house and began working as a waitress at a hotel not far from the oil refinery that spewed fumes day and night. I was seventeen.

"You need to get out of here," my friend Noel told me. He was home from college for the summer. We sat on a picnic table in a park at the edge of town, our feet on the seat, watching the sun go down, drinking Coors from pale cans. In the desert, the wind always blew. The fine dirt got in your eyes and your teeth; it crept into your clothes and left a layer on everything. But it also created beautiful sunsets.

"You're a good artist," he said. "You should be in college."

"I can't even afford a bus ticket out of here."

Like Noel, most of my friends were gone, off to chase their dreams, many off to college. A few had stuck around, taking jobs at the refinery. Noel was right. My life wasn't in this dying desert town.

"Have you ever thought about writing a book?" I asked. Noel was a big reader, and over the years we'd shared and discussed a lot of fiction.

"A novel?" He sounded excited. "How long would it take to write something like that?"

"If I wrote a page a day, I'd be done in a year."

"Wow. A year." We both turned to the flaming sky.

"A year is a long time," I said. "A really long time."

"But a book. That would be amazing. I know you could do it."

"It's a silly thing to think about. Like saying I want to fly to the moon." But men did walk on the moon, and one moon-visiting astronaut had been from Artesia.

"I know where you can get a car," Noel said. "For nothing." At my puzzled expression, he continued, "A friend of the family has a car they want to get rid of. A student abandoned it in their yard when the college folded. He's never coming back."

I wasn't surprised to learn that a spoiled kid had left his car behind with no more thought than he'd give to leaving a battered suitcase.

"It's an MG. The top is missing, but I guess it runs. You'd have to apply for an abandoned-car title, which could be a little tricky."

The whole thing seemed too good to be true, but it wasn't. I got the car, and within a few weeks I quit my job and told my landlord I was moving. Noel came to see me off. As I pulled away, I could tell he wished he were coming along, while at the same time he was thankful and relieved that he wasn't.

I ended up back in Albuquerque, where I worked at a Levi Strauss factory sewing pockets on jeans until I could no longer take the mindless drudgery. From there I went to Santa Fe, where I worked as a secretary for a propane company. I had high hopes for Santa Fe, a good place for an artist. I would save my money; I would go to school. But at the same time, I missed the Midwest. I missed my grandmother.

When the letter arrived from my uncle inviting me to come and work with him at the bar, I was on my way, never guessing that his hastily scribbled note would prove to be the most important thread in my tenuously strung-together life of cause and effect.

CHAPTER THIRTY-NINE

I could read Adrian much better now, but not all of the time. I still felt he harbored a secret self none of us would ever know. In the middle of the night, I would wake up and lie very still, and I would feel his sadness in the bed beside me.

I thought the path his life had taken, I thought his inability to stand up for himself and be his own person, weighed heavily on him. He could have been much more.

One night he must have heard my breathing change and realized I was awake.

"I'm never going to grow old," he said.

Fear shot through me before I reassured myself. Strange notions came in the middle of the night. I'd been victim to odd predawn fears myself. "Don't say that. Why do you say that?"

"I just know."

"Don't you feel well? Is something wrong?"

"I feel okay."

He was young. He was healthy. "Then why would you say such a thing?"

"I just know. I'm not even going to reach middle age."

I would have dismissed it as a lingering mood left over from a dark dream, but he seemed to have some strange connection to things I couldn't see or feel, even though I'm a perceptive person. His voicing a prediction of his future made it seem more real, and I worried that the words would somehow make it true.

A person can argue about such things and call them nonsense, but he believed, and the belief itself was painful and sad and frightening.

He didn't say anything else, but I sensed that he was already missing us. Already sad to be leaving us behind.

CHAPTER FORTY

On Saturdays, I took Alexander and Lucia to Burlington for music lessons. They both chose to play electric guitar, something that mortified Ruth. One day after practice, the children wanted to stop by their grandmother's house to show her what they'd learned.

Lucia removed the purple guitar from the gig bag, and Alexander plugged in the amp. They both sat down on the gold couch, their stocking feet on the green shag carpet, while Ruth and I sat across the living room in matching recliners. Winter sunlight poured in windows that stretched from ceiling to floor, and I tried to imagine what the room had looked like when dead bodies had been laid out for wakes. People said the house was haunted. I'm not sure I believed in such things, but Adrian still acted odd whenever I asked him about ghosts, as if he knew something he didn't want to admit.

As usual, Adrian's father wasn't home, and I sometimes forgot he lived there. He was a shadow that lurked in the orchard and in the outbuildings as he spent his waking hours hiding from his wife. I'd spoken less than ten sentences to him the entire time Adrian and I had been married.

The performance was brief, one song each, with feedback that left Ruth pressing her hands to her ears.

"Why don't you play the piano?" she asked. It wasn't the first time she'd mentioned switching instruments. "A piano is much better," she said with false enthusiasm that was meant to sway the kids. "What are you getting out of playing a silly guitar? What can you do with a guitar?"

"We could be in a band," Alexander said. At thirteen, he had an uncanny way of pinpointing a person's dislikes and driving them a little bit crazier because of it.

"A band with matching uniforms?" Ruth was hoping for the best of a bad scenario.

He laughed. "A rock band." The only thing worse would have been if he'd told her he was going to work for the Environmental Protection Agency.

"Oh no!" she said, horrified. "You don't want to be in that kind of band! Maybe a marching band. A marching band would be okay."

Alexander frowned. "I'm not going to be in a marching band."

Even as an infant, he'd been hardheaded. He knew what he wanted, and nobody could dissuade him. Unlike Lucia, who was a social butterfly and couldn't wait until she'd started school, Alexander was introverted and had spent every morning of first grade clinging to the kitchen wall, screaming that he couldn't walk. No amount of cajoling could convince him there was nothing wrong with his legs. He was even known to have pulled the stunt in school, but he'd always made a miraculous recovery in the evenings and on weekends and holidays. Considering that first tough year of school, I was just glad he wasn't living in his bedroom.

"Farmers aren't in bands," Ruth said.

"Maybe I won't be a farmer," Alexander told her.

"Come on." I got to my feet, hoping to avoid and divert the drama that Alexander was intentionally trying to create. "Time for supper. Let's go home."

"You *will* be a farmer," Ruth said. "An apple farmer. This farm will be yours one day."

"I might not want the farm," he said.

Ruth looked at me, then pushed her feet against the floor to start her chair rocking. "Guitar playing is wrong. I don't know why you allow it. I'll buy them a little piano if you don't want to spend the money."

"Even if they wanted to take piano lessons, we don't have room for a piano." A year ago we'd added on to our tiny house. Alexander and Lucia now had their own bedrooms, but the house was still tiny and we were still living on top of one another. There was no room for another toy or another piece of furniture, and we'd taken to storing our excess belongings in one end of the old salesroom, the area that had once been a blacksmith's shop.

"And if I'm not in a band," Alexander said, "I'm going to be a professional hockey player." He didn't like the idea of his life being dictated by his grandmother, and he never missed the opportunity to let her know she couldn't boss him around.

Ruth was full of fear, and I felt sorry for her because of it. I couldn't imagine being so frightened of everything. She'd once confessed that the wind scared her. And everything we said, everything we did, every choice we made, upset her. It was almost as if she saw a tomorrow we couldn't see and was constantly trying to change it. Or did the things she feared the most have a way of becoming her life? Was she creating her own future?

At ten, Alexander had still been infatuated with the orchard. He'd followed his grandfather everywhere, he'd gone on trips with both grandparents to visit apple orchards around the country, and he'd worked alongside his grandfather and father to plant new trees. But Ruth had pushed him too hard, and she'd reminded him of his responsibilities to her and the farm too many times. You couldn't push Alexander.

"Don't worry, Grandma." Lucia, now ten, zipped the soft guitar case while Alexander unplugged the practice amp and wound the cord. "I'm never leaving," she said in an attempt to comfort her grandmother. "I'll take care of the apples if Alexander won't."

"You'll get married," Ruth said, failing to understand that she'd been grooming the wrong person for orchard duty. "Hopefully you'll marry a local farmer and stay in the area. That way you can stop by to see me every day."

"I'm not going to get married," Lucia said. "I'm going to stay here forever."

As if to prove her point, Lucia spent the following year going about the farm, leaving her stamp on everything. She scraped moss from giant slabs of rock, creating letters three feet high so her name could be seen from the road. She left her signature on barns. She painted her name on sheds and gates. She scratched her name in apple trees and printed it on apple crates, sometimes adding a little daisy or heart. Her name showed up on wooden orchard ladders and in chalk on sidewalks. If cement was poured, her name was there, along with a handprint, making sure everyone knew she wasn't going anywhere.

CHAPTER FORTY-ONE

Adrian's father developed a case of pneumonia he couldn't kick. He was sent in for a series of tests. Lung cancer that had metastasized to his brain.

"People will talk," Ruth said. "They'll say it was the spray from the orchard."

It was always the farm and the reputation of the farm that was more important than the individual. The farm no longer existed to support and sustain the owners; it had become something the owners guarded and protected. It wasn't working for them; they were working for it, keeping its secrets, building it up, making it more than it was because their self-worth and identity were tied to it. Without the farm, the owners would cease to exist. The farm made them who they were, and they would keep its secrets.

People who've never lived on a farm romanticize farm life. But people who grew up on a farm and perhaps still live on a farm romanticize it more. They guard it and protect it and pretend it's more than it is. They hide its dark secrets, burying them so deep that they no longer know the truth. They don't think about the future. They don't think about what will happen and who will be hurt.

This, is how we live. This is how we do things. It's how we've always done things.

They're lulled by the gentle and harsh passage of years. They're hypnotized by the way the wet slabs of black earth fall away from the sharp edge of the plow blade, and the way the pattern of the cuts follows the contours of the land.

Repetition.

The turning of the soil.

Even the chemicals that saturated everything became in some strange way a part of the poetry, the man-made intrusion of death in nature.

Like a chant. Like rocking.

A succession of days that were never questioned.

Animals to be fed and cared for. Crops to be grown. Rain or sunshine. Life or death. The ground was always there. A promise and a curse.

There was immeasurable comfort in knowing that this would be the rest of your life. And there was immeasurable sorrow in knowing that this would be the rest of your life.

In knowing that when you were gone, the plow would still cut deep into ground you once planted. Fields that had been everything to you would still exist after you were gone. Maybe not in the same way. Maybe not with the same poetry, but they would exist.

Farmers spent their days planning a year ahead, yet at the same time, there was this feeling that they all lived in the desperate moment, with no regard for the past or the future. When something broke, they came up with a new fix. Once the topsoil and subsoil were gone, they used twice the fertilizer. There was a national crime going on in the heartland, and nobody cared.

We might have been breathing poison and eating poison and drinking poison, but so was the rest of the country. They just didn't know it.

In an odd way, the people who lived far from farms, the people who idealized farm life, were also to blame. They weren't as guilty as the farmers, but city dwellers didn't want their romantic notion of farm life shattered. They wanted to believe that the farms of their grandparents really existed. Even from the outside, the mind had a hard time separating emotional idealism from dollars-and-cents reality.

During apple season, families came in sweeping waves so that children could see where apples were grown. Parents wanted their children to experience nature and touch a piece of their own history. And I'm sure on those sweet fall days, they weren't thinking about farm chemicals.

In the salesroom, apples were sliced and offered as samples, but workers weren't allowed to wash the apples before cutting them. That might taint the warm, fuzzy feel of a trip to the orchard. Nobody wanted to be reminded of why their apples didn't have spots on the skin, or worms inside. They just wanted an unblemished and beautiful apple.

But weren't we all after the sublime?

Doctors offered no cure for Adrian's father's cancer, but over the next two years he underwent two complete rounds of chemotherapy and radiation, spending blocks of time at Mayo Clinic in Rochester, Minnesota, coming home and resting before the next visit. Sadly, he could no longer hide from his wife. The old instinct was there, and he occasionally managed to slip away to the orchard, but she always found him and brought him home.

He lost his appetite, and I baked pies for him. Apple pies and chocolate pies and lemon meringue, lemon meringue being his favorite. His memory had been damaged by radiation, and he forgot he wasn't supposed to like me. On afternoons when I kept him company in order to give Ruth a break, we chatted about the children and the farm and the always-popular topic of weather.

"How's your grandmother?" he asked one day.

Fifteen years had passed since her death. "She's fine," I said.

He nodded, pleased to hear it. "She's quite the character."

It wasn't as if he'd had a lobotomy, because the core person was still there. Anxiety and stress and worry and negativity had been lifted from

him. He was content. He was nice to me, he was nice to his grandchil-
dren, he was nice to his son. Not because he knew he was dying and
thought he'd better shape up. No, at some point during the radiation
he'd forgotten about his impending death, forgotten that the treatments
were just a temporary fix, and nobody told him differently.

CHAPTER FORTY-TWO

I lay in bed and listened to the sprayer.

It roared like a jet engine.

So many nights I used to visualize Adrian's dad out there by himself in the orchard.

Now it was Adrian.

When he reached the end, the sprayer shut down. I imagined the tractor turning in the dark, getting into position for the next row. The motor engaged and the roar began again.

The orchard wasn't close, but it took a lot of power to shoot poison over the tops of apple trees.

Odd that I found the sound of the sprayer comforting.

The windows were open, and I caught a whiff of pesticide. It had a pungent, garlicky odor that was now as familiar as the scent of fabric softener.

Fortunate son.

There was a deep dread in my heart, a dread that was always worse in the middle of the night.

The chemicals were all around us. In the clothes and sheets and towels I removed from the line. In the air we breathed and the water we drank.

We were all Lily.

CHAPTER FORTY-THREE

Adrian's father died in late summer, two years after his initial diagnosis and a few weeks before harvest.

The funeral was held at a nearby church, and the burial was in a treeless cemetery surrounded by fields and backed by a hog lot. During the graveside eulogy, I heard hogs snorting and metal feeders clanging while the smell of manure drifted over the crowd.

I found myself wondering if the hogs would always be there behind the cemetery. Maybe someone would rotate them out and put in crops. That would be nice. Well, not nice, but at least less awful.

Ruth dominated her world, and gentle spirits were especially at risk. She held people under until they gasped for air and succumbed to her will.

The death of Adrian's father left Ruth in complete control of the farm. It was her shining moment, almost a fairy tale come true. A woman born into unimaginable poverty, now the owner of one of the most impressive farms in the county. Rags to riches.

Adrian took on most of the orchard responsibilities, but he wasn't in charge, and every decision was okayed or vetoed by his mother, usually vetoed. He worked eighteen-hour days with no breaks. He went to bed exhausted and got up exhausted. He baled hay and vaccinated cattle during the day; at night, he sprayed the orchard.

"You can't go on like this," I told him. "The farm is at least a three-man operation."

I'd brought him a thermos of water, and we stood in the middle of a hay field, the waiting tractor and baler a few feet away. He'd already made twenty-five large bales, with about the same number to go. "You need to hire someone to take care of the orchard," I said. It was a solution that didn't exist.

"Who? Someone with a degree in orchard management? That would be worse than training a person from scratch."

A local farmer couldn't be hired because nobody in the area had any experience with orchards. One mistake or bit of laziness could ruin the crop for the season or ruin the trees forever. Right now Adrian was spraying for codling moths. In a few days, he would apply something that inhibited rust and mildew. Next week, it would be something else. And even if someone could be found to help, the concern—which nobody would mention—was whether or not it was ethical to allow an outsider to spray these chemicals. The risk might be worth it if the farm belonged to you, but to bring someone in and pay him minimum wage while he bathed in toxins day in and day out—it was wrong.

Alexander toiled alongside his father whenever he wasn't at school and whenever the job didn't involve pesticide. Lucia and I helped where we could, but with my writing deadlines the largest part of the labor still fell upon Adrian.

He lost weight, and lines appeared on his face. He smoked twice as much, and in his fatigue he disregarded what few precautions he normally took.

He was in his late thirties, but it was hard to see the beautiful boy in the exhausted man. Even a normal amount of farming caused people to age at an accelerated rate. Kids who'd been handsome quickly took on the appearance of emaciated street people. Hair turned gray overnight, and teeth fell out. The physical and mental stress never let up, taking a toll on the body and mind.

Every day farmers got out of bed because animals were waiting to be fed. No matter how brutal the weather, no matter if it was a weekend or Christmas or twenty below zero. No matter if you had the flu or broken ribs or a fever. When evening came, chores were repeated. When morning came, chores were repeated.

Every day was a marathon with never a chance for the body to heal or recover. It made old men out of boys, and eldest sons worked for pennies a day with the promise that the very thing that had made them old before their time, the very thing that had killed their fathers and grandfathers, would one day be theirs.

The Orchard

CHAPTER FORTY-FOUR

The spring after Adrian's father died our luck seemed to change. The Sweet Melindas bloomed, and their blossoms smelled sweeter than the blossoms of any other apple trees. Bees were trucked in, the white hives stacked and lined up behind a row of the young trees. Would they produce apples this year? They had blossomed before, and they had smelled sweet before...

I spent hours walking through the Sweet Melindas, willing the bees to pollinate the fragrant blooms. The trees were more than fifteen feet tall, their size a visual testament to the passage of time. The blossoms eventually faded and dropped, the beekeepers returned to collect their bees, and we waited. And we watched. Below the dying blooms, tiny green apples appeared.

The curse had lifted.

The darkness that had dwelled in my heart for so long was gone, replaced by hope. And even when we weren't laughing, the days had a new buoyancy. Throughout that summer, Adrian brought fruit from the Sweet Melinda trees home until the kitchen windowsill was lined with green apples picked at various stages of growth. At night, reaching blindly for a lamp, I'd knock a pippin to the floor, where it would roll under the bed. Days later, I would follow a trail of dust to find the shriveled Sweet Melinda. At bedtime, Adrian unzipped his jeans and apples fell from the pockets, hitting the braid rug with muffled thuds.

"You won't have any apples left to pick once they're ripe." I spoke in a soft voice because the children were asleep beyond our closed door.

"There's no need to worry about picking them all." Adrian removed his T-shirt, tugging it over his head, dropping it on a chair. "I've never seen so many apples for a first harvest." He was trying to sound casual, but he couldn't mask the excitement in his voice. "I'm really just thinning, and if I don't thin, the branches will break. The trunks could even split, so I have to make sure the trees aren't bearing too much weight."

I'd seen how Adrian had fashioned crutches from dead trees to help support the load.

"If we don't have any big storms, we should have a bumper crop." He turned out the light.

"What color will they be?" I asked. "The Sweet Melindas." Color was directly related to temperature. I'd also learned that soil unique to locale gave apples a distinct flavor. Two identical trees, one in Washington State and one in Illinois, would not produce apples of identical flavor. The apples from the Curtis farm had more flavor than apples grown in most other parts of the country. The flavor was hard to identify because it contained hints of so many things, and describing it could be compared to describing wine. Words like *earthy* and *flowery*, *woodsy* and *loamy*, always came to mind.

"Red." The mattress dipped. In the dark, Adrian reached for my hand, linking his fingers with mine.

"What shade of red?" I was aware that I sounded like an eager child, curious about the world. I felt young again, new again.

"Color is tricky. You want the temperature to briefly hover above freezing about a week before harvest. Just a kiss. If that doesn't happen, if temperatures remain high, the color won't be as rich. A good apple crop also depends on the right amount of rain. You don't want a lot of rain before harvest. The apples grow too quickly and will be mushy."

"What kind of red would make you happiest?"

Adrian and I often talked about the orchard, about what we would do if we were running it. Maybe it was because he was now a father, but over the years he'd come around to thinking that organic might be the way to go. We read everything we could read about organic farming, and dreamed of a farm where we would grow apples that weren't without flaws and where toxins didn't drift in open windows.

Over time, Adrian had implemented what subtle environmental measures he could get away with, that wouldn't cause friction. Planting waterways to stop soil erosion, creating wildlife habitat with brush piles, leaving saplings and hedgerows for migratory birds, fencing off streams and ponds so cattle couldn't pollute. Small measures, but important ones.

He unlinked his hand from mine, shifted to face me, and began stroking my thigh. "I like a true red."

"With a blush?"

"No. No blush. I want a solid, unbroken red."

"What about shape? Round? Oblong? Bumps on the bottom like a Delicious?"

"Round like a Winesap, but with shiny, thin skin."

I hated the rough, sandpaper skin of a Winesap but knew it was natural armor. "Isn't thin bad?"

"On an insect level, but it's a risk I'm willing to take for skin that's flawless." He reached under my cotton shift. The vintage gown he'd given me the night I'd tried to run away was long gone, damaged by time and years.

I could smell the wallpaper in the room, and I could smell the mustiness behind it. Not a bad smell. An odor I associated with another era and other people who had died long ago. Sad pioneers who never smiled. And even though I couldn't see the wall, I sensed it a few feet away: solid, looming, watching—the hand-hewn timbers giving the space an organic feel.

"Does everything always have to be perfect?" I asked, letting out a little gasp as his hand continued to explore places he'd explored hundreds of times.

The window was open, and humid air drifted into the small bedroom, carrying with it the thick scent of green fields. Cicadas whirred, and I knew I would find empty shells on the screen door in the morning. Our sweet daughter kept a jar on the kitchen counter with the hollow brown bodies she collected.

The nature that existed in the dark was different from the nature that existed in the daylight. Night nature hypnotized me. Lulled me into thinking everything would be okay, that it was there to protect and nurture. Instead of being vast land and sky that went on for miles, it held us close; it sheltered us.

"Do you have something against perfection?" Adrian asked as he slid the gown up my body. I lifted my arms, and the fabric was gone. Damp air caressed my bare skin, and then he was pressing down, covering me, his body hot, as if he'd spent the day gathering and storing heat from the sun.

"No..." My breath caught, then released. I could taste the saltiness of him on my lips, feel the movement of muscles under my fingertips. "Not always."

CHAPTER FORTY-FIVE

The weeks passed, and with every storm we held our breath. Once the rain stopped, we rushed to the orchard to make sure the entire crop wasn't on the ground. Storms weren't our only concern. Some apples required a longer growing season, and we didn't yet know if the Sweet Melinda was a late apple that would be threatened by frost.

In early September Adrian appeared in the kitchen, pulled an apple from his pocket, and announced that they were almost ripe.

The fruit wasn't quite full-size and hadn't yet reached the deep red we were both hoping for. He rummaged in a drawer and found a paring knife, grabbed a cutting board, and sat down at the kitchen table. I took a seat opposite him, elbows on the narrow wooden surface. This was the way to do it. With ceremony.

He placed the apple in the center of the cutting board. It sat there by itself without rolling or pitching, slightly flat on the bottom, the shape similar to that of a pumpkin. We watched it for a while, committing the moment to memory. And then, with steady fingers, Adrian tipped the apple on its side and made the slice, separating the fruit into a top and bottom half.

"When you cut it this way, the seeds make a star pattern."

Reverently, he opened the apple to reveal the seeds and the star. The meat of the apple was almost luminescent, the white surrounded by a thin line of red. I don't know if I'd ever seen anything quite so beautiful, and in that moment I understood the reward for seeking perfection.

He offered me the top half. I accepted it and raised it to my mouth.

"Wait." He looked alarmed by my impatience. "Smell it. You have to smell it." He demonstrated, lifting the other half to his nose while closing his eyes. He inhaled. I did the same. It smelled sweet and earthy. Kind of woodsy. We opened our eyes.

"What do you think?" he asked.

"Lovely."

"We have to wait another minute. See if it stays white. That's important."

And so we waited.

Later, he examined his piece. "A little yellowing, but not bad. Now smell it again."

I lifted the apple section to my nose. "It has more of a floral scent now."

"That's because it's already breaking down."

We both took a bite, laughing at the mirror image we presented, and the dual sharp snap as our teeth broke the crisp skin. The apple wasn't quite ripe, yet it had an incredible flavor, like a combination of wine and cherries.

"Oh my God," I said. "The best apple I've ever eaten." And it was.

He smiled and nodded, then quickly finished his half.

"Don't eat the seeds!"

He laughed. "They won't hurt me."

I guess it only seemed right that he would eat the whole thing.

"Chicken," he said, watching me nibble around the core.

"I'm not swallowing any seeds, no matter how special the apple."

And then we both got to our feet and began acting silly. Laughing, giddy.

He wrapped his arms around me and pulled me close. "You know the whole country is going to be talking about these apples, don't you? Maybe we'll be able to build a log home in the woods."

"Or move away? And start a farm of our own?"

He pressed his lips to mine, then looked at me. "That too."

But I could see the hesitation in his eyes.

It actually made me sad to think about going somewhere else with the Sweet Melinda trees. I imagined hauling infant trees in the back of the truck, their roots wrapped in burlap. Planting them in some foreign soil in Michigan or Wisconsin. I don't know why that felt so wrong and made me so sad, but it did. Like Adrian, the trees belonged to the farm. We all belonged here.

CHAPTER FORTY-SIX

"They're ready."

Adrian came bursting into the house, radiating heat from the sun, smelling of diesel and fall leaves and late grasses and drying cornstalks soon to be combined.

He'd made a satchel from the flannel shirt he'd removed once the day had warmed up. Now he untied the sleeves and tails, letting six apples roll across the table. Two metal picking baskets were stacked in the corner. Once we determined that the apples were truly ripe, Adrian and I planned to strap on the baskets and harvest the trees ourselves, carefully removing one apple at a time.

I grabbed the cutting board and handed a paring knife to Adrian. They were his apples; he should make the first slice.

"Wait." I'd almost forgotten the wine I'd picked up for just this occasion. I removed the cork from the bottle, then poured the burgundy liquor into two glasses that we raised and touched together.

"To us and the Sweet Melindas," I said. The pure and delicate chime of glass against glass echoed in my head, seeming to predict a future that was clear and bright.

This time Adrian placed the knife next to the stem and sliced down through the core, the blade making solid contact with the cutting board. The two halves separated and rolled apart.

We both stared at the sliced apple. At the dark, rotten core and the worm shifting in a brown tunnel. I can't explain the kind of dread I felt in that moment. It was similar to the day when I'd eaten the mushroom and thought I was going to die. Fear. It was fear. But an odd kind of fear. Not the kind of fear you feel when something startles you. Not the kind of fear you feel when you almost step on a snake. This fear was deep. This fear went all the way to the bone.

"Codling moth," Adrian said.

I knew it; he didn't need to tell me.

I picked up one half and examined it. "I don't even see a spot. I don't even see where the worm entered." I thought of all the nights spent spraying, all the nights Adrian had carried pesticide back home on his skin and clothes, crawling into bed too exhausted to shower.

He grabbed another apple and sliced it open. Same thing. One by one, he sliced open the remaining apples. They were all damaged.

I pressed fingers to my lips. Tears burned my throat and eyes. "Can they be saved? Is it too late?"

He shook his head. "I don't know. Maybe. Maybe not."

We got in the truck and drove to the Sweet Melinda trees. We slipped into the picking baskets and in silence we began to harvest the infested crop, hoping to find at least a few apples that weren't damaged.

Adrian pulled out a pocketknife and began slicing open random apples as he tugged them from the tree. Every one was infested.

He shrugged out of his harness and tossed the metal basket to the ground. "Stop picking."

While the straps bit into my shoulders, I curled my fingers around the lip of the metal basket and stared at the apples. Round and beautiful. And the smell. Sweet and slightly mysterious, the red contrasting beautifully with the gray of the battered container.

"The trees have to go," Adrian said.

I looked up in alarm. "No."

"They'll infest the rest of the orchard."

He was overreacting. He had to be overreacting. "Can't you spray?" I couldn't believe I was suggesting spray. "With something stronger?" Maybe the secret spray. The spray he had hidden away, the spray his father had stockpiled.

Now I finally understood how it happened. The desperation to save something you've worked so hard to create. The length you find yourself willing to go, the compromises you're willing to make. Just this once.

I ducked my head as he helped me remove the basket from my shoulders. He dropped it to the ground, and apples spilled at our feet. Beautiful apples, red against green.

I looked up at him through a haze of tears. "I'm sorry."

He reached for me, pulling me close. "It's okay. They're just apples."

But they were more than just apples. We both knew that. "You have to spray," I said. "Now. Right away."

I felt his fingers in my hair, against my scalp. "No."

"Yes."

"I've done enough spraying."

Back at the house, I poured the wine down the drain and it stained the white sink.

Adrian appeared with a shovel. "I'll bury them."

It took me a moment to realize he was talking about the apples.

He dug a hole in the backyard, tossed in the apples with their rotten cores and pale, writhing white worms, then covered them with dirt.

The next day, he bulldozed the Sweet Melinda trees and used the blade to push the trees into a giant pile in the middle of the orchard. He doused the trunks and branches and beautiful red apples with gasoline. Then lit a match.

The fire burned for almost twenty-four hours. By morning, all that was left were a few smoldering embers, but the sweet scent of burning apple wood permeated our clothes, our hair, our house, and I wondered if it would ever go away.

Over the next few days, Adrian and I didn't talk about the trees, and we tried to find pleasure in small things. On Sunday afternoon while the kids were visiting friends, I packed a picnic basket and we went fishing in the pond behind the house. Maybe if we forced ourselves to engage in a relaxing activity, joy would follow.

CHAPTER FORTY-SEVEN

The bobber vanished. Adrian jumped to his feet and turned the crank, reeling in the line. No longer a boy but a man, strong and healthy. A week had passed since the bulldozing of the apple trees, and time hadn't yet done much healing, at least not for me. It wasn't the failure of a dream that left me feeling stricken; it was knowing the trees would have given Adrian a voice, given his ideas weight and validation. His mother had humored his experiment, but now he needed to get down to the business of real crops.

But I didn't want to think about the politics of the farm. I wanted to enjoy the afternoon and the feel of the sun on my face. I was a lazy fisherman, more interested in everything that went along with fishing than I was in catching a fish. I watched sleepily from a blanket, hoping my hook no longer had a worm. Earlier I'd searched for four-leaf clovers and had found soft beds of four, five, and six leaves.

Adrian snagged the fish with his free hand and brought it close.

It was covered with oozing sores. Tumors.

The loss of the Sweet Melindas seemed suddenly insignificant. If a single moment could define a life, then this was Adrian's moment. And if a single moment could forever change the way I viewed the world, this was mine. In that instant we both felt the future pressing down on us.

He removed the hook from the deformed mouth and looked across the water to the orchard. "Chemicals are getting in the pond."

Proof. Finally proof.

"Let's go back to the house." I didn't want to be here anymore.

They'd lost track of why they were farming. It should have been about making a living and supporting your family, but somewhere along the way, that core reason had become buried and maybe no longer even existed. It was more about big business and success on a large scale, no matter what the cost, no matter how it impacted the very people it was supposed to support.

Silently we packed up everything. Adrian gathered the poles and I grabbed the picnic basket.

It was like the moment you found out someone had died. Before the bad news and after. You were occupying the same space, but everything looked different and was permanently altered. Two different worlds.

"We can't stay here," Adrian said. "As soon as the crops are in, we'll start looking for new ground."

"Where?" I was no longer the person with outsider ideas who couldn't exist on a real farm. We both understood that something had to be done. Things had to change. But as long as his mother ran the farm, we believed change would never happen.

"Up north. Minnesota or Wisconsin."

A place where the land was less contaminated, the air purer. A place where an organic movement was taking hold. I thought about our children. I thought about Adrian and me.

Hopefully it wasn't too late.

Even though we were deep in harvest, Adrian and I found time to pore over farming magazines and the monthly newspapers that arrived advertising farms for sale. We found three possibilities, all small acreages, two in Wisconsin and one in northern Illinois, near the quaint down of Galena.

"Let's drive up and look at them as soon as the apples are picked," Adrian said. "I should be feeling better by then." He'd been running a low-grade fever, and he was on a second series of antibiotics.

I was surprised that he was actually initiating his plan, and I had to wonder if he could make himself go through with a transplant and the guilt that would come with leaving. He hadn't thought it out, and once he did...well, he might see there was no satisfactory solution. He might see that he was trapped. Leaving his mother alone with the orchard would be a lot of guilt for a firstborn son to carry. But there was no harm in looking, and the trip itself might give us both a fresh perspective. "We'll make a family vacation out of it," I said. "We could visit House on the Rock."

"And maybe Frank Lloyd Wright's Taliesin in Spring Green."

Adrian called the listing numbers, and I made motel reservations. But two weeks later, when the apples were in crates and stored in hillside bunkers, when the cider press was running and the corn hadn't yet been picked, everything changed.

CHAPTER FORTY-EIGHT

The eldest son is born into two things: a life sentence and a death sentence. The fall harvest had just begun when Adrian's doctor told him he might have cancer. He was next in line; this was his destiny. But it was too soon. Years too soon. Four years had passed since his father's death, and Adrian should have had more time.

Fear is bigger in the predawn hours.

I think that's when our emotions are most vulnerable. In our sleep, a door opens to allow the dreams inside, and along with those dreams come the emotions that play such an important role in our sleeping life.

I set the alarm, but there was really no need. Adrian and I were awake most of the night, those few moments when we would sink into sleep the only relief from worry and dread.

It was a two-hour drive to Iowa City and medical specialists, and the sun rose as we headed north. The light washed away the stars and exposed the dirty windshield. Farmers were in the fields picking corn, trying to beat the rain.

*　　　*　　　*

The diagnosis ended up being what we most feared. Cancer.

"Was it caused by smoking?" Adrian immediately asked. He didn't want to think he'd done this to himself and his family.

"It's almost unheard of to see throat cancer in someone who just smokes," Dr. Wagner told us. "There's always a second toxin."

"Pesticide?" I asked.

"No research has been done on the connection, but I can tell you we're seeing more and more farmers with this type of cancer." The doctor looked sad.

Upon learning that Adrian was an apple farmer, Dr. Wagner had been full of questions, and the two men quickly bonded over talk of the apple trees the doctor had recently planted. Even doctors seemed to need to embrace apples as a symbol of family and the perfect life.

"Operating is the only treatment," Dr. Wagner told us. "But the cancer is extremely advanced, and your chances of a cure are low. I'm sorry."

Adrian chose to have the surgery, but before he was out of the hospital we both sensed it had been unsuccessful, and we soon had confirmation of our suspicions.

Dr. Wagner took us to his office, shut the door, and asked us to sit down in the matching chairs on the other side of his desk. Behind him on the wall were framed magazine covers proclaiming his department to be the best in the country. I found myself thinking that medicine hadn't really come very far in the past one hundred years, that the big advance had been in creating a false sense of shiny new medicine, when in reality doctors were still torturing patients until they died. Not that Dr. Wagner was to blame. He'd done everything he could.

Next to the magazine covers were framed photos of his kids, taken in what looked like a suburban front yard, plus pictures from the exotic locations doctors seemed to like to visit.

Dr. Wagner fiddled with his pink tie, and Adrian and I could both see that he was struggling for composure in order to give us the test results. I think he'd become fond of us and had connected in ways he probably shouldn't have.

"The cancer is still there," Adrian said, helping the doctor along. The news would be no surprise, but devastating nonetheless.

"Yes. I'm sorry."

"What do we do now?" I asked.

"In forty percent of cases, chemotherapy will slow down the growth for a maximum of three to six months," the doctor told us. "Then it will become totally ineffective. There is no cure, and in sixty percent of cases it will do nothing but make the patient sick. That's all I can offer you."

His words sucked the air out of my lungs and caused the room to shrink to a pinpoint. I was aware of my heart slamming in my chest and aware of Adrian sitting beside me, but nothing beyond that. For that moment, the rest of the world didn't exist.

"I'm not going to get the chemo," Adrian said, his words no surprise. "If there's no chance of a cure. How long do I have to live without it?"

"Two weeks to two months."

Two weeks. I'd been expecting a year, maybe two or three. "Fourteen days? How is that possible? He seems fairly healthy." Just that morning he'd fed cattle and repaired a broken fence. I mustn't have heard correctly.

"Part of the tumor is wrapped around the carotid artery. That artery could burst at any time, and if that happens the patient bleeds to death. It might sound unpleasant, but it's fast and painless. If the artery doesn't burst, the tumor will slowly poison the patient."

I'd known this day was coming, but that made it no easier. Adrian had known too. Almost a lifetime, it seemed.

From him I sensed an initial fear, followed by acceptance and relief. *This is it. This thing that has followed me my whole life.*

He'd been in such a hurry to marry and have children. For years, he'd felt the shadow of his short life looming over him. And it almost seemed he'd been anxious to experience everything in a condensed time frame.

I thought of the occasions when he'd alluded to his own death. *I'm never going to grow old. I'm not even going to reach middle age.* He'd spoken with such conviction. And now here it was. The end he'd been waiting for, that he now seemed ready to embrace.

"How are your apple trees?" Adrian asked, breaking the silence that had fallen over us.

Dr. Wagner blinked in surprise, then said, "Great. Had a little trouble with rabbits, but we wrapped the trunks and that seems to be working."

Adrian nodded, glad to hear it. "Do you know the apple tree is part of the rose family?"

"No," Dr. Wagner said. "I didn't."

We got up to leave. Dr. Wagner stood too, his expression stark. I could see the pain in his eyes. I think he thought he'd let us down, and oddly enough, I wanted to comfort him. *You did your best.* But the words seemed inappropriate.

"I wanted to go into research," Dr. Wagner said. "But my professors told me I could do more good as a surgeon." He was doubting his choice. As a researcher, he would never have had to tell someone he was dying.

"Good luck," Adrian said. And he meant good luck with the apple trees, and good luck with his family, and good luck with the next patient he couldn't save.

They shook hands. "Good luck," Dr. Wagner said, and he meant good luck with dying.

I was too upset to drive; Adrian drove us home. Calm. At peace. As if a weight had been lifted from his shoulders as he gave himself up to his own destiny. He reached across the seat and took my hand. "I'm sorry."

I threw a tissue on the floor, adding to the pile growing at my feet. "Dr. Wagner made it clear it wasn't caused by cigarettes alone." I didn't know that many farmers, but I knew four who'd been diagnosed with throat cancer in the past few years.

Adrian gave my hand a comforting squeeze before letting go. "No matter what caused it, I'm sorry."

I knew he meant he was sorry for leaving us, sorry for smoking, sorry for not being able to fulfill our dream of moving. The idea of our own farm had kept him going, but I don't think he could ever have left Curtis Orchard and his birthplace. I think that's where his sense of peace and relief came from; dying solved a lot of problems. Moving wasn't the only way to leave a place.

That day he became more than the farm, more than his mother's son. He took a step toward something none of us could see. He'd finally reached a point where nobody could force him to do what he didn't want to do. He'd never been in control of his own life, but by forgoing the chemotherapy he would at least be in control of his own death.

Once we were back home, we told Alexander and Lucia the news.

"You're not going to die on my birthday, are you?" Lucia sobbed. "Don't die on my birthday!"

In two weeks, she would be fifteen.

"Does that really matter?" Alexander asked. He wore brown Carhartt coveralls, and his face was red from hauling hay on the tractor. Up close, he looked more like me, but from a distance, if they were crossing a field, father and son couldn't be told apart.

"I don't want to think of it every year on my birthday," Lucia explained as she struggled to stop crying.

"She has a valid point," Adrian said with a smile. I could see he was trying not to laugh. "Okay, I won't die on your birthday. How about that?"

"Oh, I don't care!" she said. "I don't want you to die at all!"

"Come on." He wrapped his arm around her. "It'll be light for another two hours. Put on a pair of boots and we'll go for a walk in the woods."

As the four of us walked through the woods, we were thinking that this was the last time we would walk these paths together. And somehow the knowledge made the moss that bordered the streams that much greener and made the air that much sweeter. And it made the day the saddest day on earth, but also the most beautiful.

The sun was going down by the time we broke out of the dense timber, ending up in the north end of the orchard.

"This is one of the original plantings," Adrian said. We stood at the foot of the towering and twisted tree where I'd harvested Transparent apples years earlier, shortly after my grandmother had died. From where I stood, the orchard represented five generations of Curtis men, two of them standing beside me. The oldest trees had been placed in the ground by Adrian's great-grandfather, the youngest by Alexander.

Adrian pulled off a piece of bark and showed us where the codling moth had bored into the trunk of the ancient tree. "The old orchard needs to be destroyed," he said. "All of it. It might be too late, but it's the only way to possibly save the newer dwarfs."

"I'm not staying," Alexander said. "Once you're gone, I'm not staying. I'm here for you and Mom, not her." Of all of us, Alexander had suffered the most verbal abuse from his grandmother over the years. Her bullying would have been forgivable if it had been an isolated incident. But Ruth was terrified of being left alone, so her insults had never stopped.

"Once I'm gone, all of you have to leave," Adrian said. His words were something we already knew, but he needed to speak them. He needed to remind us. He needed to make sure Alexander, Lucia, and I would do what had to be done.

It seemed wrong to talk of leaving when we knew Adrian wouldn't be coming with us, but at the same time he was seeking reassurance about our future without him.

We'd been remiss in not establishing our own life, our own home, from the beginning. It could have helped carry us through this hard time, but instead we were squatters, stewards, with twisted roots that had never taken hold the way they should have.

"Does anybody have a pocket knife?" Lucia asked.

Alexander pulled a knife from his Carhartts and handed it to her. She opened the blade and carved her name in the trunk of the tree. At first I didn't understand why she still felt a compulsion to leave her mark on everything, especially when we would soon be gone. But then I realized she had every right to leave it wherever she wanted. This place belonged to her as much as it belonged to anybody. And I thought, how right for all of us to carve our names in a dying tree that had been part of the original orchard.

Ruth didn't take the news of Adrian's untreatable cancer well. In fact, she unraveled before our eyes.

That's the sad thing about a life of pretense and a life designed from magazine ads. The people in those ads didn't die from cancer, and they didn't have to deal with heavy issues. It was all Tupperware parties and cupcakes. It was all cigarettes that were good for you, and cars that didn't kill. Innocent children could drink herbicides with no consequences. Bad things didn't happen in her world, and death was the first thing Ruth had come across that she couldn't control.

CHAPTER FORTY-NINE

When word got out that Adrian hadn't long to live, people stopped to see him one last time. The visits were awkward as guests wrung their hands, stared at the floor, and struggled to find the right words to say to a dying man. One of the visitors was Connie.

The years hadn't been as hard on her as they'd been on Adrian. Standing outside on the front step, she didn't look much different from the day she'd appeared at the door with the gift of the rolling pin. She'd gained weight, but her hair was the same, and she could have been wearing the same clothes—a testament to how nothing ever changed here.

I joined her outside in order to give Adrian a chance to prepare for her visit.

She looked at me with mild affection. "I never thought you'd last a year, yet here you are. Shows what I know."

People always go on about how quickly time passes, but on a farm it stops, the vanishing landscape the only way to mark the years. Time stood still for everyone except the dying.

"We never made that apple pie," I said. It may have been an odd thing to say, but I'd discovered that the mind latched on and clung to past vignettes when focusing on the end of a life.

"People are saying Adrian isn't going to be buried with his father and grandfather," Connie said. "They're saying he's going to be buried at South Henderson. That can't be right. Nobody's been buried there in years. As far as I know, they don't even allow burials anymore."

Yes, nothing changed. Connie had once again ridden in on gossip. She was here to get the scoop.

"We found a plot owned by Adrian's ancestors," I told her. "There were two empty spaces." The cemetery was isolated and serene, with hills and huge shade trees, surrounded by timber. "I got in touch with the board, and they gave us their okay." Adrian and his mother had been fighting about it ever since. Where he would be buried was his one and only real act of defiance, and it would come after he died.

We went inside, and Connie kept her visit light. She was one of the few who understood that she was there for Adrian and that he was living moment to moment. It wasn't his place to reassure and soothe or tell her everything would be okay.

He could no longer talk, and he kept a pad within reach, the rasp of pencil lead moving across paper another reminder of what could have been.

He and Connie joked about grade school escapades, and when he grew tired, Connie got up to leave. Her lips never trembled. Her eyes never filled with tears. She smiled, blew him a kiss, and walked away. Moments later, I looked out the window to see her sitting in her red truck, forehead against the steering wheel.

Once she was gone, Adrian flipped the tablet to a fresh sheet. But this time he didn't pass the message to me so we could carry on a conversation. He wrote with intensity and mystery, and when he was finished I took the tablet from his hand.

A confession. Written with a pencil that had sketched people and animals and trees, now telling a different story, a detailed story of the pesticides Adrian and his father had applied over the years, and, the most chilling of all, how his father had disposed of the canisters.

Everybody does it.

As far as you're concerned.

At last I knew the secret Adrian had carried for so long, and because he entrusted me with it, I knew he loved me. He was leaving it up to me to reveal what he'd shared if I so chose. He was leaving it up to me to do the one thing he could never have done even if he hadn't become ill. Death would give him a voice.

I put the tablet away and handed him a new one.

CHAPTER FIFTY

Adrian lived four months, long past Lucia's birthday. Doctors said the unexpected length of those final days was most likely due to his years of hard labor. His body wouldn't shut off.

When you spend weeks watching someone die, you reach the point where the end seems more of an idea than anything that will really happen. But one night after Adrian had been moved to a Burlington hospital room overlooking the Mississippi River, his breathing changed.

Long and deep, with only a few inhalations per minute.

I wanted to take his hand. I wanted to talk to him, but I was afraid the slightest touch, the slightest shift in air, would call him back.

Fly away. Just fly away.

Leave that rotting body and fly, beautiful, perfect boy with the golden curls. Fly far, far away.

I held my breath, afraid to move or make a noise. From somewhere came the faint sound of a television, and I could hear soft voices from the nurses' station.

It seemed that only a single growing season had passed since the day Adrian had walked into my uncle's bar, and yet we had two beautiful children. A son. A daughter.

The passage of time is ephemeral. You wrap it up and put it in that place where memories go. And when you pull it out, it doesn't matter if it's one year or eighteen. It feels the same.

As I watched Adrian's slow, labored breathing, I remembered the day he'd finally spoken up, not for himself, but for his son.

There had been talk about Alexander joining his grandfather in the orchard, where he could learn how to spray and how to make perfect apples.

"Absolutely not," Adrian had said. "He can't spray apples or corn."

"He has to learn someday," Adrian's father told him. "He can't be a farmer if he doesn't know how to spray crops."

"I don't want him around any chemicals."

"You're babying him."

Then Adrian had taken his young son aside and told him to say no. "If your grandfather tells you to spray, don't do it. He's not your boss. He's not your father. I'm your father, and I'm telling you not to do it. You don't have to."

Alexander had looked at his father with relief. And he'd looked at his grandfather with shame. But he didn't spray.

Love doesn't happen overnight. It doesn't happen in the first months of attraction and infatuation. In that moment when a father finally takes a stand, not for himself but for his child, that's where love is shaped and redefined in a way I could finally understand.

Adrian took one long breath and slowly exhaled.

A minute passed.

Another breath. Another exhale.

Now he was the one lying in bed waiting to die. At the nurses' station, two dark heads were bent over a book. Moments later, a lovely woman in yellow beachcombers entered the room and offered Adrian a plate of mushrooms. Or was that a dream? And were they apples?

He ate them all. Every last one. Because that's what good boys do.

And then he was gone.

A life unfinished.

He hadn't accomplished what he'd wanted to accomplish, always thinking he had time. Always thinking his turn would come.

Don't wait.

Don't ever wait.

Two hours later, after all the paperwork was signed, I drove home.

The moon reflected off the river, and when I reached the bottoms, I could smell the fields on both sides of the road.

I didn't meet another car.

The house was dark, the children asleep.

This had never been our house, and it had always felt wrong. Like us, it existed to serve the farm. It now gave off the emptiness of death and the aura of biding its time until the next occupants, the next caretakers, arrived.

Inside, I lay down on the bed and waited for dawn.

CHAPTER FIFTY-ONE

With the hired man anxious to move into our house, I packed. A year later his wife would be diagnosed with cancer. You have to wonder if it was from the spray he carried home on his clothes. Or spray that floated in the windows as they slept.

I opened the funeral guest book. One of those awful designs. White, gold letters, puffy. And there was my uncle's strong signature. I hadn't seen him, but the church had been crowded. I heard he had stomach cancer, probably caused by drinking water from his shallow, hand-dug well. I would visit him soon.

I was surprised to find that Adrian's belongings filled a few small boxes. That was it. His books and his sketch pads full of drawings. I'd saved most of the tablets he'd used when he was dying. Maybe someday I would read them again. Or maybe not. I'm not sure I'll ever want to relive those days with that kind of intensity.

As much as he'd hated it, his world had been the farm. Not the house. Not even us—not really. He wouldn't have bought a farm up north.

Death was the only way he could leave.

Now that he was gone, the farm was different. Lifeless and empty.

When he'd been alive, it had held possibilities. Now it was just ground. Just a farm. Just the place that had killed him.

CHAPTER FIFTY-TWO

Three weeks after the funeral, I found us a place to live, a house outside Burlington with a barn and four acres for Mr. Red. We couldn't possibly leave him behind. A few days before moving from the farm, I stopped the truck in front of what used to be the stable and blacksmith's shop to deal with something I'd been dreading—retrieving our stored belongings. I'd deliberately chosen a time when the salesroom was open and people were around, hoping to get in and out without Ruth knowing I'd even been there. Thankfully, the door was unlocked, and I began carrying boxes to the truck.

Five minutes into the task, Ruth materialized from behind parked cars. "What are you doing in here? Get out!"

I suppose I should have called her, but I hadn't spoken to her since Adrian had died, and I was afraid a phone call would give her enough warning to make sure the door to the storage area was locked. "I'm just getting our stuff."

"*Stuff.*" She mocked me by exaggerating the word, a word that, to her mind, belonged to hippies and bohemians and uneducated morons. "You don't have any *stuff* here." The disgust and hatred in her face reminded me of the day she and I had first met in this very driveway. Her opinion of me hadn't changed in eighteen years.

"I do have stuff here, and I'm getting it."

Her thoughts shifted from her dislike of me and my vocabulary to Adrian. "I didn't do anything wrong!"

When her son had needed her most, she'd said horrible things to him, things no mother should say to her dying child. Apparently she was suffering from guilt and maybe a little remorse; otherwise, why would she bring up something so out of context?

"You're a coward!" she'd screamed at him. "You're dying on purpose! You're dying to get away from me and the farm!"

He'd been the bravest person I'd ever known. But the words she'd spoken had held a seed of truth, because dying was the only way he would have ever left. He'd felt some measure of relief knowing it would all be over soon, and that had enraged her.

She tried to block my way; I stepped around her.

"Let me see! Let me see what you're taking!" She followed me and pawed through the boxes in the back of the truck, making sure I wasn't stealing anything of hers.

Ten minutes later, Ruth changed her tactic and began dragging large items out of the building and into the driveway. She was a pack rat, and she'd salvaged a lot of my old junk over the years, most of it ending up in the storage area.

"Take it! Take all of it!" she said. "I don't want anything of yours!"

An audience was growing in front of the salesroom; workers and customers had come outside to see what the ruckus was about. Ruth was aware of the audience too, and began to put on a show.

"Oh, you've been so cruel to me! So cruel!" she wailed. "I've done nothing to you! I was always good to you! I treated you like a daughter!"

True, I thought, thinking of my mother. I put the last box in the truck bed, slammed the tailgate, and opened the driver's door.

Behind me I heard something heavy dragging across gravel; I turned to see Ruth standing near the tailgate, a wooden headboard in her hands.

"Take this!" she shouted.

"That's not mine," I told her, braced to climb into the truck. "I gave it to you."

"What am I going to do with it?"

I fixed Ruth with an unblinking stare. I no longer had to tolerate her. I no longer had to take anything from her for the sake of keeping the peace, for the sake of her son.

For some people, things seemed to happen in threes. For me it was twos. Two crazy mothers. The first one taught me that family ties meant nothing without love and mutual respect. Blood or marriage was no reason to endure mental or physical abuse. From now on, I would surround myself with people who loved me, not people who hated me. People like Ruth would no longer be a part of my life.

By her smug expression and her confidence in the moral support gained from the witnesses in front of the salesroom, I could see Ruth fully expected me to obey her by loading the headboard, but I stayed where I was. "What should you do with it?" I asked conversationally. She leaned closer in anticipation of my submission. And then I followed up with the last words I intended to ever speak to her: "Shove it up your ass."

The audience let out a collective gasp. I hopped in the truck and drove away, Ruth and the headboard and her gaping mouth framed in the rearview mirror.

CHAPTER FIFTY-THREE

We drove away and didn't look back. Had Adrian married me because he knew I was not like them, that I would find the strength to do just this if the time came? I'll never know. But I couldn't shake the feeling that we'd left him there.

Nobody in his family cared about the land the way he had cared. His mother saw it as a business, while he'd seen it as nature. He'd known every curve, every dip, every glen, every stream, every tree on the farm.

Sometimes I think he's still roaming through the timber, and sometimes I imagine him riding Mr. Red, or driving the David Brown tractor through a field. But mainly I imagine him walking through the woodland that he loved. And I think about what could have been.

The codling moth won. And I've been told the entire old orchard was bulldozed, the trees burned. I wouldn't know, because I haven't been back. I've heard that the only trees left are the more disease-resistant dwarfs. I've been told that fences have been ripped out and the waterways Adrian struggled so hard to maintain were plowed. The fields eroded so that now plantings and green waterways have vanished to reveal gaping wounds that will never heal.

You can't control nature; you have to work with it.

Trees and migratory habitat are gone, and the wind constantly blows across miles of barrenness, carrying away the little remaining topsoil.

Like the scraps of paper Adrian used for drawing, the land and farm had been his canvas. Most of his small environmental efforts are now gone. Wiped out.

The farms of our grandparents no longer exist. People don't want to hear that, but farms are big business. They are no more warm and fuzzy than a factory is warm and fuzzy. Somewhere in the seventies, people got off track. And it wasn't just the farms. I think about all of the dying small towns; I think about the beautiful Victorian homes torn down to make way for the four-lane highways that will take people to strip malls on the other side of town.

As a culture, we seem to need to make our own mark in our own time, even if it's the wrong mark. Even if the picture is without flaws, the next generation feels the need to add their own signature, while the people sounding the alarm are considered crazy and foolish. In the mid-eighties in rural America, it was uncool to worry about the environment. It was uncool to worry about spray and chemicals.

Our children won't be farmers, but they will be what Adrian couldn't be. Artists. Teachers. World travelers. Because they did what Adrian couldn't do.

They left.

But they will always remember the smell of earth cut deep with the sharp edge of a plow blade. And they will remember the sound of the wind in the corn. On long winter nights they'll remember...and go back in their minds.

If you drive down Highway 34 and see a narrow lane that drops away from the main road, you'll have found the old highway. Locals call it Bogus Hollow because counterfeit money was once made there. But now it's just broken buildings covered in tangled vines. An old rope swing. Decayed barns, abandoned wells. Silent and secret.

Beyond Bogus Hollow lies Curtis Orchard.

Don't slow down.

Don't even hesitate.

Just keep driving. Past the place where the sprayer still shoots chemicals over the apple trees and where, on hot, humid nights, corn still smells like dark, mysterious perfume. Where ginseng grows in shadows, and bluebells still bloom on hillsides too steep to plow.

A place that goes on without us.

CHAPTER FIFTY-FOUR

Minneapolis, Minnesota

I turned off the interstate and took the exit ramp to downtown Minneapolis. Seven years had passed since we'd left the farm. After Adrian's death, Lucia and I moved to the place I'd found for us, and Alexander left for college. Once in Burlington, I avoided crossing the Mississippi, and I almost convinced myself that hundreds of miles lay between our new place and the orchard.

The writing money I'd squirreled away for years supported me, and new book contracts came along. I was used to a minimalist lifestyle, and starting over hadn't scared me. Once Lucia entered college, once Mr. Red was gone, Alexander and Lucia talked me into leaving Iowa. I followed them north to Minneapolis, land of the Spoonbridge and Cherry, Foshay Tower, Weisman Art Museum, Dinkytown, and Bob Dylan.

I'm a city girl again. I ride the light rail, and I sit in cafés and drink lattes. My new friends don't know about my past, and when I tell them I used to live on a farm, they laugh and say, "Yeah, right."

I don't like to leave the city. Beyond its boundaries are cornfields and pastures and orchards, painful reminders. And I won't eat apples or drink cider. It's not the spray; I can't bring myself to ingest a symbol of a failed life.

I turned into Dayton's Ramp, pushed the red button, and pulled the ticket from the automated machine. The arm rose and I circled up, parking on the fourth floor. I took the elevator to street level, then made my way along the wide sidewalk. It was Saturday night and couples were everywhere, heading to restaurants and bars.

At the corner, I pressed the pedestrian button. When the green WALK light appeared, I checked for traffic like any seasoned city dweller and crossed the street to First Avenue, the club Prince made famous in *Purple Rain*. I passed the main door and slipped into 7th Street Entry, First Avenue's smaller venue.

"I should be on the guest list," I said.

The tattooed door girl checked her paper, found my name, and stamped the back of my hand.

Inside, as my eyes adjusted to the dark, I found a spot in the corner and watched the room fill. Two young guys settled to my right, and their conversation was easy to overhear.

"Do you know anything about this band?" one of them asked.

"They're brother and sister," the other guy replied. "Can you imagine being in a band with your sister? That would suck so much."

I smiled to myself.

And then Alexander and Lucia took the stage. It was their first gig. Lucia had just graduated from college, and Alexander was a sought-after recording engineer. Beautiful children, beautiful people, the last of the Curtis line. They'd both waited a long time for this moment, but no one in the room knew how long, or how far they'd traveled to get here.

It was an odd feeling to know that this wouldn't be happening if Adrian hadn't died. The three of us wouldn't be standing here in this room, in this space, in this city.

Many of the song lyrics were about the farm. Strange how we'd wanted to get as far away from that life as possible, we'd wanted to escape any chance of daily reminders, and yet all three of us were using art to express and re-create and revisit the past.

Heritage.

The farm would always be ours, even if we were no longer there. We would claim it in writing, in music.

Fear makes you brave. Fear makes you fearless. We left our terror back there in that old life, and here in this world everything was new even though it didn't ring with the same brutal and beautiful authenticity of soil and crops.

Alexander and Lucia finished their set and put down the guitars. With a bouquet of red roses in my hand, I squeezed through the cheering crowd and headed for the stage.

Acknowledgments

The Orchard was difficult to write. It was hard to revisit that dark place and immerse myself in it for months at a time. Once the story was finished I went on a short quest, but the agents I queried didn't want a memoir; they wanted thrillers, Anne Frasier books. Most didn't even want to see the material, so I gave up and tried to forget about the project that meant so much to me. A year later I decided to try again and submitted the memoir to Marly Rusoff, of the Marly Rusoff Agency. I simply wanted to be able to say I'd done all I could do in order to put *The Orchard* behind me and move on. That didn't happen. Marly read the material and said it was an important book, a brave book. She believed in something I no longer believed in, and a few months later *The Orchard* sold to Deb Futter, my wonderful editor.

I want to thank my family and friends for putting up with my dark nature during a period of my career when I grappled with failure. I especially want to thank my agent, Marly Rusoff, and my editor, Deb Futter, for getting it, for recognizing and understanding what I was trying to say, for embracing my dream.